DOW
THEORY
REDUX

THE CLASSIC INVESTMENT THEORY REVISED & UPDATED FOR THE 1990's

Michael D. Sheimo

PROBUS PUBLISHING COMPANY
Chicago, Illinois

This publication is designed to provide accurate and authoritative information in regard to the subject matter covered. It is sold with the understanding that the publisher is not engaged in rendering legal, accounting or other professional service.

Library of Congress Cataloging-in-Publication Data Available

ISBN 1-55738-081-3

Printed in the United States of America

1   2   3   4   5   6   7   8   9   0

Dedication

To Linda, My Most Important "Indicator"
My Best Investment Advisor

Contents

Preface

The Dow Theory has been with us for more than a century. During that time it has evolved somewhat, most notably through the refinements and additions of William Hamilton in the 1920s and further clarification by Robert Rhea in the 1930s. The Dow Theory has long had many users, some who follow its concepts to the letter and others who make only partial use of it. The purists tend to be the analysts, sending out their well studied reports to investors and advisors. The more flexible Dow theorist is usually a stock trader; either an institutional investor or an individual who invests on a regular basis. These investors tend to rely on several sources of information: news, market indicators, economic indicators, the Dow Theory or other "technical" systems. They make use of these systems based on a certain amount of flexibility, as well as discipline. This enables them to control the system rather than allowing the system to control them.

This book explains the Dow Theory, technical analysis, fundamental analysis, and other market indicators. Chapter Three looks at the evolution of the market and the Dow averages, discussing the difficulties in trying to compare the market of 1989 (or the 1990s) with the market of 1929 (or any other year). They are all radically different markets.

Other stock market indicators are examined in Chapter Eight— how they work and what they may be saying in terms of current market strength and direction. The book examines the Dow Theory from a current perspective, where a bear market can last a few short weeks and a bull market can be attaining new "relative highs" rather than achieving record high levels.

Important changes, such as increasing volume and volatility, are examined. The "condensing effects" created by increased volume, changes in trading strategy, leveraged buyouts and other activities are discussed in Chapter Four.

Today's rapidly changing market makes it more necessary than ever before for the individual to be aware of indicators and other market information. To know the indicators—to understand how they work and what signals they are giving—is the only way the investor can hope to achieve investment objectives. That many investors are becoming aware of this situation is shown by increased interest in personal computer trading systems, as discussed in Chapter Fourteen.

Even with a computer system it is still necessary to work with the market indicators in order to read the signals generated. Whether the investor is a "buy-and-hold, long-term strategist" or a "short-term trader," the indicators can help the individual plan and implement a more effective, more profitable investment strategy. *The Dow Theory Redux* can help provide this knowledge.

Acknowledgements

I would like to thank my colleagues David Huss and Eric Erickson for their encouragement. I thank Lynne Bly and John Harrington for helping me take control of the words. I also thank Willy Mrosla for giving me better insight into how a computer can provide useable information to an investor.

Michael D. Sheimo

Chapter One

The Dow Theory: The Origin

Around 1901, articles began appearing in *The Wall Street Journal*, which gave opinions on investing in the stock market. These articles contained information on how to choose stocks, how to limit risk and how to understand the movement of stock prices. The ideas set forth in these articles were those of Charles H. Dow, co-founder of the Dow Jones & Company and the first editor of *The Wall Street Journal*.[1]

Charles Dow indicated that his conclusions regarding the stock market were based on more than fifteen years of observation of the market and on his charting of the stock price movements. Dow considered price tracking important to an investor's understanding of individual stocks and the stock market as a whole. In fact, stock price tracking was important enough for Dow to simplify the activity for readers of his newspaper. He did this by creating the Dow Jones Railroad Average (now called the Transportation Average)[2] and the Dow Jones Industrial Average.

Dow's purpose in creating the averages was two-fold: to create a list which would be an indicator for the entire stock market and to create a list which would be representative of all the stocks traded. But in Dow's time, the accomplishment of his purpose was not an easy task.

In the late 1800s, while it was already well-recognized that stock prices tended to move as a group, the market was not as active as it is now. Many stocks would sit for days without being bought or sold. Newspapers listed all of the daily trading prices of selected stocks, a feat which now would be impossible. Finding stocks which traded with regularity was also quite difficult. To find stocks which could be considered "representative" of all other stocks increased the problem.

These problems were solved by constantly reviewing and changing the lists. Now, nearly one hundred years later, the lists are still being changed and adjusted. For instance, a company on the list may be bought out by some other company, or the basic business of a company may change dramatically or the stock may no longer be representative of the stock market and removed. As a result of continuous changes like these in the market, the lists of market averages are in a constant state of revision.

In summary, Dow studied the stock market and formed a basic movement theory, then created lists of stock market averages to illustrate this theory. These lists were then adjusted and refined to be representative of the entire stock market.

The market averages, as well as the Dow Theory, would be further refined by other editors of *The Wall Street Journal*, (predominantly William Peter Hamilton, editor from 1908-1929) and market devotees such as Robert Rhea (author of *The Dow Theory: An Explanation of Its Development and An Attempt to Define Its Usefulness as an Aid in Speculation*, published by Barron's, 1932).

Throughout this study it will be important to remember that the Dow Theory can be helpful in forecasting certain trends, but it is not infallible. However, understanding and working with the elements of the theory can be of assistance in planning and implementing an investment strategy.

Primary Trend

A primary trend is a bull market, moving in a steady upward direction, or a bear market, steadily dropping. Primary trend determination is the most important concept to understanding the Dow Theory. Although it is a simple concept, trend determination can vary in complexity. For example, does the chart in Exhibit 1 represent a bull or a bear market?

Exhibit 1 Primary Trend

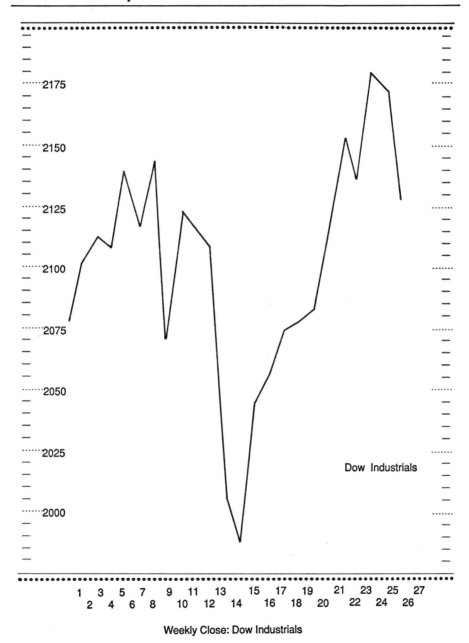

Weekly Close: Dow Industrials

At a glance, the last price is higher than the first; therefore, it appears to be a bull primary trend. That would have been small consolation to the investor who bought stock in the first week and sold the stock in the thirteenth week. Even so, the conclusion of a bull primary trend is correct.

Charles Dow might have taken this conclusion a step further, adding that it is a continuation of a bull primary trend showing some signs of weakness in its inability to reach consistent new highs.

Later, *Wall Street Journal* editor and Dow Theory developer, William Hamilton, may have noticed that the stock market has been forming a line for the past six months. This is a period of accumulation and distribution, with slightly bull market tendencies, as is shown by repeated breaking to the upside. However, the lack of support when the market breaks to the downside will bear watching.

A modern Dow Theory practitioner might say something like this: the current market trend is definitely bullish with a tendency to correct sharply on profit taking (as shown in weeks 9 and 13 in Exhibit 1). Strongest support appears to be in the 2050 to 2075 area (as shown in weeks 1 and 9, and to some extent in weeks 15 and 16). Strong resistance is appearing at the 2165 to the 2180 levels. Stronger penetration of these areas of resistance could foretell a significant rally to new levels, perhaps 100 to 200 points before any substantial profits would be taken. Failure to penetrate the 2180 area of resistance could eventually lead to a sell off with the Dow falling back to the 2050 area or below. If the market drops and does not find the historical support at the 2050 area, it could seek lower support at or even below the 2000 level.

Notice that not one of the preceding descriptions is precise in its forecast. All of the descriptions look to the possibility of a reverse in the Primary Trend. Although there are usually signs and signals before a market reverses trend, the reversal can happen quickly. Dow, Hamilton, Rhea, and many later Dow Theory followers have stressed the fact that forecasting market movement cannot be reduced to a precise mathematical formula.

There are just too many factors to consider and too many variables which cannot be controlled for any form of stock market forecast to be completely accurate. However, stock prices tend to move as a group and the market averages tend to move in a wavelike motion. There is a Primary Trend to the stock market and it is important to recognize that trend in investment planning and daily strategy.

Determining the trend can be accomplished in a number of ways. The two basic methods are: first look at a chart of the market, if the trend is not quickly apparent, look at a longer time period; second, compare the market trend to a "flatter" chart, such as a three-month or six-month moving average. The flattened longer moving average chart is refigured each new trading day. It looks back for a 200-day trading period and calculates the average. The average removes the confusing peaks and valleys and gives a clearer picture of the trend. In Exhibit 2 we have added the 200-day moving average figures to our weekly Dow Industrials chart.

The 200-day moving average is of some assistance here, showing the primary trend to be in an upward direction. The moving average in the first one-third of the chart is misleading. It was adjusting to the severe decline of the Dow Industrials in October of 1987. This points out an important weakness of the moving average. A sharp and sudden movement of the market can make a long-term moving average unreliable for some time.

There are also other moving averages (i.e., 4-week, 6-week, 9-week) which can be consulted for primary trend determination. It may be necessary to obtain this information from one of the many newsletter services available. The shorter time period presents a more accurate picture of the current trend, but lacks the flatter, long-term view. It can be helpful to consider both long-term and short-term moving averages after extrordinary activity.

Determining the primary trend is the first and most important step in the use of the Dow Theory. This is essential to any investor who wishes to make use of stock market indicators for market forecasting. Once the primary trend is determined, it becomes necessary to determine the secondary trend.

Secondary Trend

A secondary trend is often referred to as a "secondary reaction" in a bull market, or "secondary rally" in a bear market. It is essen-

Exhibit 2 Moving Average

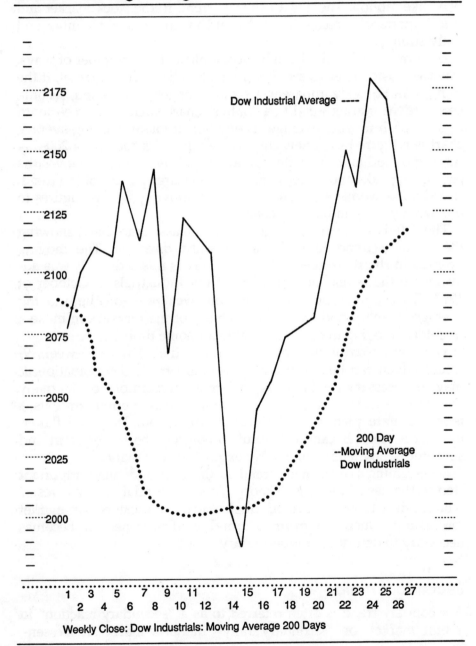

Dow Industrial Average ----

200 Day
--Moving Average
Dow Industrials

Weekly Close: Dow Industrials: Moving Average 200 Days

tially a movement of the market in a direction which is contrary to the primary trend. A secondary trend may last a short period of time, such as a day or a few days, or it may last a few months. It can be very difficult to determine whether a contrary movement is a secondary reaction or an actual change in the direction of the primary trend. Some understanding of "support" and "resistance" levels can be helpful in determining the movement of a secondary trend (See support and resistance in Chapter Seven.)

It is a good idea to be wary of forecasters who attempt to be mathematically precise in their predictions of secondary trends, too many uncontrollable variables come into play with stock market predictions. For instance, assuming the analyst is held in high regard, the market may begin to move as predicted. However, once a movement of the stock market is initiated, there exists no power which can bring it to a sudden halt. Therefore, a predicted fall may be further than expected, or less than expected. The stock market, comprised of buyers and sellers, will determine how far the market will move. This distance is not determined by an analyst, although the initial motion may be caused by the analyst or forecaster.

In Exhibit 3, one can easily see the "ideal buying range" for a short-term stock trader. Though not without risk, this opportunity occurs as the Industrial Average breaks through the six month, or 200-day moving average, and shows support. This secondary reaction took just over a week to move down significantly, then break through the 200-day moving average, bounce around for awhile and then, in the fifth week, begin to recover.

Note the support at about the 1980 level. The support is not consistently on the numbers, but there is definite support. The primary trend upward was then resumed, even though it was a bit on the shaky side.

Secondary reactions can be caused by any number of events from the strength of the dollar to simple profit taking. This particular secondary trend was initially caused by the Federal discount rate being raised from 6 percent to 6 1/2 percent.

The timing of buying and selling stock can be improved by the recognition and understanding of secondary trends in the market. the chart in Exhibit 3 shows an excellent buying opportunity for three reasons:

Exhibit 3 Secondary Trend

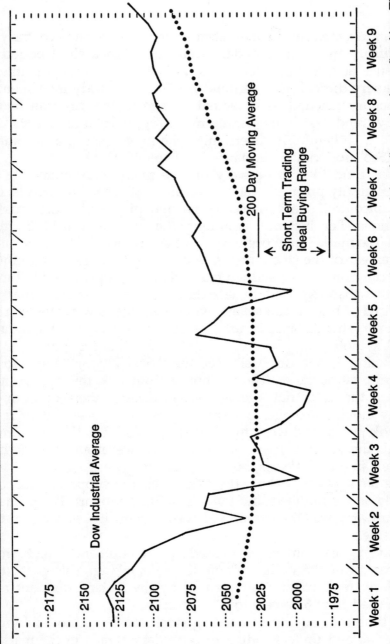

Secondary reactions can be caused by any number of events from the strength of the dollar to simple profit taking. This particular secondary trend was initially caused by the Discount Rate being raised from 6% to 6 1/2%.

1. The raising of the discount rate from 6 to 6 1/2 percent signaled the probability of a drop in the market.
2. The Dow Industrial Average broke through the 200-day moving average on a well-defined secondary trend.
3. The Dow Industrial Average broke through the 200-day moving average just as the moving average was beginning a definite upward turn. This carried with it a strong implication of likely support.[3]

The risk side is that the market could have continued to drop after breaking through the moving average. Other indicators suggested that a continued drop was unlikely. It is important for an investor to base decisions on more than just one indicator.

Tertiary Trends (Daily Fluctuations)

In the early 1900s, Charles Dow described daily price fluctuations by saying that "the surface of the market is apt to be deceptive." It was important to track daily prices to establish trends, but they were of little consequence in the determination of primary trends.

To William Hamilton, daily fluctuations were to be ignored, except when the daily figures were analyzed over a long period of time. "...the closest analysis of the fluctuations day by day, year in and year out, over much more than a quarter of a century, shows well-defined primary and secondary movements giving meaning to the third or daily fluctuations of the average price."[4]

A similar thought was put forth by Robert Rhea later in the 1930s. "Inferences drawn from one day's movement are almost certain to be misleading and are of but little value except when 'lines' are being formed."[5]

In the 1980s, daily price fluctuation takes on a new importance; now we see the Dow Industrial Average being able to move more than 500 points in a single day, on volume of more than 600 million shares traded.

(On October 19, 1987, the Dow Industrial Average closed down 508 points, at a level of 1738, on total volume of 604 million shares. A drop of more than 20 percent of its total value.)

October of 1987 was an extraordinary sequence of events with unfortunate consequences for many investors. Many investors sold early and saved money, others sold at the wrong time and lost money, still others rode their investments to the bottom and then rode them back up again. It is most important to remember that days like October 19, 1987, can happen suddenly and with little or no warning.

Exhibit 4 illustrates that unforgettable day in October. Note the rather sharp rally off the open and a second rally in the second hour of trading. Also, note that most of the real damage was in the final hour of trading. In fact, the extent of the damage wasn't known until long after the close. It took more than an hour to clear the huge volume of orders.

It was not a good day to be placing orders of any kind. As was learned later, many orders were never filled, even though they were market orders. The system was terribly overloaded.

Most trading days in the stock market are not extraordinary but are rather ordinary in their actions. The market may move about a bit, but most days are relatively calm and steady. There are days when the market drops on the open and rallies later in the day, or days when just the opposite occurs. There are days which have a slow but steady climb of a few points and days when a steady decline is in progress. And occasionally, the market goes neither up nor down, but closes for the day unchanged.

As shown in Exhibit 5, even a rather moderate day in the stock market can have some volatility. The Dow Industrials began this day with a steady move upward, with the Transportation Average moving up slowly (point A). This appears to have caused a temporary undervalue in the Transports. At 10:00 (EST), the Industrials leveled out just as the Transports began to make a catch-up move. At point B, the Industrials began to fall, just as the Transports hit a peak. Both averages then fall to points C and D at noon.

The creation of a scenario to explain movements in the stock market is almost always a guess—there are many possibilities. However, the news released on this particular day can give some clues.

Exhibit 4 October 19, 1987, Hourly Trend

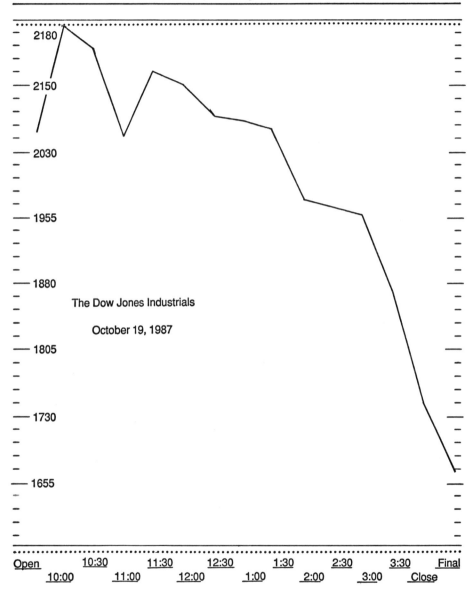

The Dow Jones Industrials

October 19, 1987

On Friday, November 25,1988, the market was down more than 17 points on light total volume of a bit more than 72 million shares. This was caused in part by the economic news of an agreement reached at a meeting of the OPEC nations to set oil production quotas and fix prices. For the stock market to be down that much on light volume was a possible technical "oversold" situation.

On Monday the 28th, doubts of OPEC's ability to stand firm on the Friday agreement were emerging. This situation and information caused an immediate rally, with the Transportation Average lagging only slightly. At midday an announcement of an increase in the prime lending rate was made public.

Even though news of the increase in the prime rate of one-half of one percent was expected, the event did have a minor impact (points C and D). After the minor reaction at noon, both averages resumed the rally, losing some strength in the last two hours of trading. The Dow Transportation Average closed up 13.12 points. This is unusual.

It is fairly rare for the Transportation Average to have a larger gain than the Industrial Average. On this day it was nearly twice as high! Most technical analysts would call this event a very "bullish signal" for the short term. The signal was tempered somewhat by the fact of light to moderate trading in total volume of just over 123 million shares.

Bullish signal it was. The following day had the Dow Industrials up over 12 points and the Transports up over seven points. In effect, the Transports pushed the Industrials to a level of alignment.

The importance of the daily movement of the stock market can be easily observed. This fact is of special interest to the short-term trader, who is interested in buying at a reasonable price and selling at an acceptable level of profit in a shorter period of time than long-term investors. Daily movement of the market is important to all investors who are in the process of placing buy or sell orders. If an investor placed a sell order at noon on November 28, the results would likely have been a disappointment when compared with either the opening or the closing.

Exhibit 5 Average Day, Hourly Trend

November 28, 1988

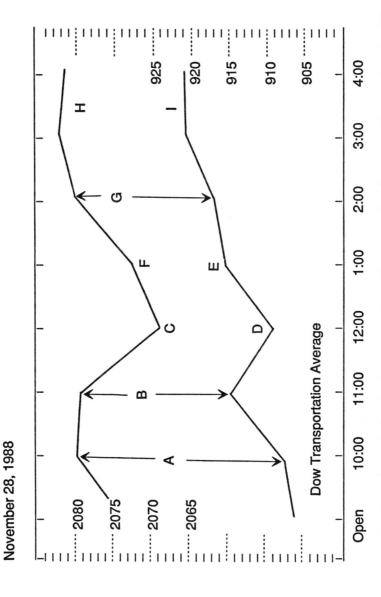

Dow Transportation Average

Hourly Movement: The Dow Jones Industrial Average and the Transportation Average. (Eastern Standard Time)

The Averages Must Confirm

Charles Dow mentioned the confirming trends in the Industrial Average and the Transportation (Railroad) Average. He never really discussed why this event would occur, but there is a certain logic to the occurrence. Industry gets the raw materials and ships the final product using transportation; profits of the two sectors are thereby intertwined. As value rises in the industrial stocks due to increased production, value will also rise in the transportation stocks due to an increase in shipping. This could be called a "fundamental" or economic reason for the two averages to confirm each other.

Another reason is more technical in nature. Professional stock traders know that the two averages are supposed to line up and confirm each other. If the averages are not in alignment, the professional trader knows that there is a bargain existing somewhere. This trader will take some risk and place orders in the stock of the "weaker" average. Then as the averages line up properly, this trader can sell for a modest profit. Sometimes a large profit. This is one form of an arbitrage play.

The confirmation of the Dow Industrials by the Transportation Average can be observed in a long-term (weekly or monthly) chart or a short-term (hourly) chart of the different levels reached by the respective averages. In Exhibit 6 a period of nine weeks is covered based on the closing levels of both averages.

Notice in the first week and a half, where both averages are falling. The Industrials seem to fall in a greater proportion than do the Transports. This is not unusual; the Industrial Average has a tendency to be more volatile than the Transportation Average. Although, as we observed earlier, this situation may create an arbitrage situation, confirmation does exist because both averages are dropping.

On Thursday of week 2, an interesting event takes place (point A). The Industrials start a well-defined rally. The Transports barely move; no confirmation of the rally. Therefore, the Industrials pull back on the next day (point B). In week 3, another Industrial rally begins, and again the Transportation Average puts forth a feeble effort. Confirmation doesn't happen this time either; the Industrials fall back to point C.

Exhibit 6 Confirming Averages

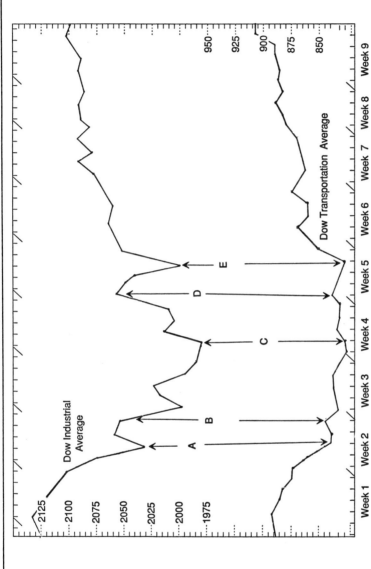

The confirmation of the Dow Industrials, by the Transportation Average, can be observed in a long-term (weekly or monthly) chart or a short-term (hourly) chart of the different levels reached by the respective averages. In the chart below a period of nine weeks is covered, illustrating the closing levels of both averages.

Once point C is reached, it is the bottom for this time period. It is the lowest point of the stock market for the past few months. Although the Transportation Average has not wanted to participate in rally attempts, it doesn't seem to want to drop much lower either. These facts, together with other information, suggest an "oversold" condition in the market—a temporary, technical condition.

The Industrials rally again, this time with only a slight hesitation, on the way to point D. But again, the Transports only give a weak attempt at confirmation. Perhaps the "oversold" idea was incorrect. Halfway through week 5, it becomes obvious that the Transportation Average will not confirm the rally by the Industrials. In fact, Transports are going south. The Industrials join in the drop. This brings point E, where the two averages finally come together.

From point E through the end of week 9, the two averages are essentially confirming each other. The confirmation is not strong, neither is the rally, but it is evident. The trend is distinctly bullish.

Trend confirmation can be a useful tool of analysis. When the trends of the Dow Industrial Average and the Transportation Average do not confirm each other, a change is likely to occur. Determining the direction of the change can be difficult, but an investor should be informed as to the situation. Confirmation can be observed in both long and short terms. Looking for short-term confirmation can be an advantage when placing buy and sell orders. (For a discussion of trend confirmation in the short term, see Chapter Four.)

Endnotes

[1] The first edition of *The Wall Street Journal*, appeared July 8, 1889.

[2] The original list of eleven stocks appeared in 1884. The two averages appeared together in 1896.

[3] This strategy represents a somewhat contrarian approach, normally dropping through the moving average is a sell signal, while rising above would be a buy signal.

[4] *The Dow Theory* by Robert Rhea, published by Barron's, 1932, page 197. From a quote by William Hamilton appearing in *The Wall Street Journal*, October 18,1922.

[5] *The Dow Theory,* by Robert Rhea, published by Barron's, 1932, page 67.

Chapter Two

Dow Theory Concepts

The averages discount everything that can be known about the financial condition of the country and, to a large degree, the world. This means the market is able to adjust quickly to any change in the economic status which could have future impact on the earnings. Signs of inflation, possible recession, or a booming economy will all be swiftly adjusted into the movement of the stock market.

Whether this is done efficiently or inefficiently, the discounting of what is known happens quickly. The investor who waits a day or a few days to take action is too late. The information has changed and the market is adjusting to new information. If information or news is to be acted upon, it must be done as quickly as possible.

Forming a Line

Forming a line is a movement of the market averages which has a small up or down variance. The averages will generally vary about five percent either side of a line, extending a few weeks to several months. This type of movement indicates the existence of accumulation and distribution of stock at the same time. See Exhibit 1, page 21.

Occasional breaks from the pattern will occur. If a break occurs to the upside, on increased volume, it is a bullish signal. If breaks are more to the downside, the signal can be bearish.

Total Volume

Total volume can relate to price movement by showing the strength or weakness of a particular move, whether up or down. When a market is showing an increase in volume, it can be a signal of building strength. A decline in volume is often showing a weakening market, one that is likely to soon be turning in direction. Constant low comparative volume for an extended period of weeks or months is on the weak side and tends to be a "lethargic market" with only minor advances or declines.

Strong bull markets tend to advance on strong volume, but as that volume begins to weaken on advances, it can signal an approaching directional reversal. Bull markets tend to begin on fairly light volume and build momentum along the way. Bear markets can begin with excessively strong volume after a strong bull advance, but will often slow and proceed in a drifting fashion, slowly dropping lower.

The best use of volume as an indicator is as a gauge of the strength of any advance or decline. Checking the up-volume versus the down-volume on any given day can also provide insight into investor sentiment in the "broad" market.

For example, if the daily volume is showing 150 million shares traded, when the average for the past six weeks has been about 100 million shares, it would show an increase from light to moderate trading. More investors than usual are interested in the stock market. If the breakdown of the volume is 100 million shares up, 25 million shares down and 25 million shares unchanged, an investor knows that there are a significant number of buyers on the scene.

Volume can be a good "broad" market indicator, taking into account all of the stocks traded on the New York Stock Exchange. A narrowing of the spread between the up- and down-volume, or an increase in the number of shares traded unchanged, can signal an approaching change in the market.

Exhibit 1 Forming a Line

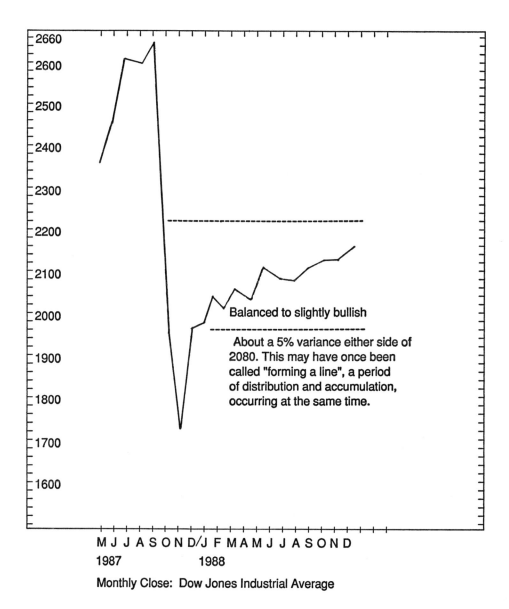

Balanced to slightly bullish

About a 5% variance either side of
2080. This may have once been
called "forming a line", a period
of distribution and accumulation,
occurring at the same time.

M J J A S O N D/J F M A M J J A S O N D
1987   1988

Monthly Close: Dow Jones Industrial Average

Double Tops and Double Bottoms

Double tops and double bottoms have traditionally been regarded as an interesting phenomenon, but with little forecasting value. Charles Dow mentioned them and he was perhaps misunderstood as to his conclusions regarding their significance. Dow's concern would not have necessarily been the double top or double bottom, but rather the inability of the averages to attain new highs, therefore the market may be turning. In a bearish market, the support indicated by a double bottom can indicate the approach of buyers to the scene.

In 1926, William Hamilton made a totally incorrect market forecast, when he predicted a bear market, based on the appearance of double tops. The bear market, Hamilton predicted, did not occur until three years later in 1929.[1]

Multiple tops or bottoms should be noticed, as they do show levels of resistance or support, but they should be looked at as only part of the picture.

Stocks Tend to Move as a Group

Stocks tend to move as a group. This is one of the few market conclusions with which virtually everyone agrees. Mathematical analysis of stock price forecasting has frequently been proved and disproved. The forecasting validity seems to depend on which theory of investing being presented by the analyst.

A great deal of time, energy, and money has also gone into the laborious study of the validity of market forecasting. Most of the time spent was wasted on the obvious: There are just too many variables. Even a small amount of common logic points out the improbability of accurate, consistent, precise market forecasting. There are hundreds of thousands of variables, based on individuals' perceptions and sentiments, none of which can be controlled. However, stocks do tend to move as a group.

Manipulation Does Exist

Manipulation does exist in the stock market and it is likely to continue. Some manipulation falls within the boundaries of legality and some does not. In the past couple of years evidence has floated to the surface indicating large scale, illegal trading schemes based on "insider information." This is but one form of the many types of manipulation in the stock market.

Flurries of activity can often be observed just prior to important announcements. These flurries may be based on speculative or lucky guesses, or they may be based on the dubious attainment of pre-announcement information. Whatever the source of information, the fact is these "flurries" of activity seem to be correct many times.

The appearance of unexpected activity can be a speculative indicator. However, the placing of trades by the individual investor can be filled with a high degree of risk. This risk is particularly true of smaller, lower capitalization stocks. The activity may in fact have been induced in order to allow the large investors a fast exit.

There are various degrees to which certain types of manipulation can take place:

- Manipulation of individual stocks can be relatively easily accomplished.

- Manipulation of secondary trends is possible to some degree, although it can cause an unpredictable reaction.

- Manipulation of daily trends occurs, but again this is often more by influence than control. It may be compared to a car sliding on the ice. There is the controlling influence of the brakes or the gas pedal, but there is little or no control of the final outcome of the slide.

- Manipulation of the primary trend is not likely to be possible.

Dow Theory Main Concepts

Primary Trend

The primary trend is the most important trend, as it is the dominant long-term trend of the stock markct. It is generally measured in months and years.

Secondary Trend

Secondary trend can occur at any time. Secondary trends proceed in a contrary direction to the primary trend. Secondary trends are shorter term and are usually measured in days, weeks, and sometimes months.

Tertiary Trend

The daily fluctuation of the stock market. Charles Dow, among others, believed daily trends to be of little or no importance. These trends have gained importance in recent years.

Averages Must Confirm

The Dow Jones Industrial Average and Transportation Average must confirm each other in trend determination. This confirmation does not necessarily occur at the same time, or even on the same day. A lack of confirmation can be an important signal of weakness, gathering strength, or an impending change in direction.

The Averages Discount Everything That Can Be Known

That is, everything known about the financial condition of the country, and to a large extent, the world, is discounted.

Forming a Line

A period of accumulation and distribution of stock, where the market averages fluctuate within a small range. If breaks of the trading range occur, it is bullish when they break to the upside, but bearish if they break more often to the downside.

Volume Can Relate to Price Movement

Volume is a broad market indicator which can show the existence of strength or weakness in a particular move. The up volume and down volume figures can be an indication of overall market sentiment.

Double Tops and Double Bottoms

Tops and bottoms, whether doubled or tripled, can be of technical significance, but tend to be misleading when considered alone.

Stocks Tend to Move as a Group

This is true of the market as a whole and is also true of different industry sectors.

Manipulation Does Exist in the Stock Market

To some extent it can be observed, but it can seldom be counted on for a specific move of an individual stock or the market as a whole.

ENDNOTES

[1] *The Dow Theory*, by Robert Rhea, published by Barron's, 1932, p. 94

Chapter Three

Dow Evolution

A number of important historic events occurred in the year 1884.

- Alaska became organized as the District of Alaska.
- The cornerstone for the Statue of Liberty was laid on Bedlow's Island in New York Harbor.
- Grover Cleveland received the Democratic nomination of President and was elected in November.
- Mark Twain's, *The Adventures of Huckleberry Finn*, was published.
- *The Customer's Afternoon Letter*, published by the Dow Jones & Company, added a new component to their financial newspaper.

This new publication was a list of the stocks of nine railroads and two industrial companies. The average price of these stocks was presented in a fixed point, rally and decline fashion. The list's average price movement was called a "market average."

This first Dow Average came into being on July 3, 1884. The companies on that list were:

Chicago & North Western
Delaware, Lackawanna & Western

Lake Shore
Louisville & Nashville
Missouri Pacific
New York Central
Northern Pacific Preferred
Pacific Mail Steamship
St. Paul
Union Pacific
Western Union[1]

Dow Jones & Company had been established a couple of years earlier (November of 1882), by Charles Dow, Edward Jones, and Charles Bergstresser. The three had been working together at another financial publication, the Kiernan News Agency. They left to form their own financial information company at 15 Wall Street, next to the New York Stock Exchange. The *Customer's Afternoon Letter*, provided daily bulletins on financial matters to interested subscribers. The little paper was quite popular with investors on Wall Street and it continued publication until July of 1889.[2]

The Wall Street Journal

On the evening of July 8, 1889, the *Customer's Afternoon Letter* ceased publication to give way to a new four-page financial information newspaper called *The Wall Street Journal*.[3]

The *Journal* had a new "more easily read" format, and more complete information than was available from other sources at that time. An interested person could obtain a copy of the new paper for the sum of two cents. A truly serious investor could purchase an annual subscription for the reasonable price of five dollars a year. The paper contained four pages of financial news and data on bonds, commodity quotations, active stocks, railroad earnings, and bank and U.S. Treasury reports.

Dow Jones & Company saw a need for accurate, complete financial news reporting. They saw a special niche and filled it with a reputable newspaper. The first issue of *The Wall Street Journal*, also contained a lead article on "The Average Movement of Prices." This was the kind of information which would bring the newspaper into prominence. This is the way that lead article in the first issue looked:

Average Movement of Prices

The bull market of 1885 began July 2, with the average price of 12 active stocks 61.49.

The rise culminated May 18, 1887, with the same twelve stocks selling at 93.27.

Prices gradually declined for about a year, reaching the next extreme low point April 2, 1888, the 12 stocks selling at 75.28. The movement since then, counting from one turning point to another, follows:

Last low point	Apr. 2, 1888, 75.28
Rallied to	May, 1, " 83.54
Declined to	Jun. 13, " 77.12
Rallied to	Aug. 8, " 85.95
Declined to	Aug. 18, " 83.76
Rallied to	Oct. 1, " 88.10
Declined to	Dec. 5, " 81.88
Rallied to	Feb. 18, 1889, 87.77
Declined to	Mar. 18, " 83.59
Rallied to	June 12, " 91.38
Closed Sat. night	July 6, " 87.71

(Source: *The Wall Street Journal,* July 8, 1889, p.1)

It was quite clear, with this first issue, that the market averages would form an integral part of *The Wall Street Journal.* The average would continue to develop until it actually became "the market."

If this early list of average price movement representing turning points were placed on a line graph, it would look like the graph in Exhibit 1.

It is readily observed that this is an early form of what is now called "technical analysis." These turning points actually represent areas of "support" and "resistance," two important indicators in modern Dow Theory forecasting.

Exhibit 1   First Market Average

Dow Jones "Market Average" Turning Points

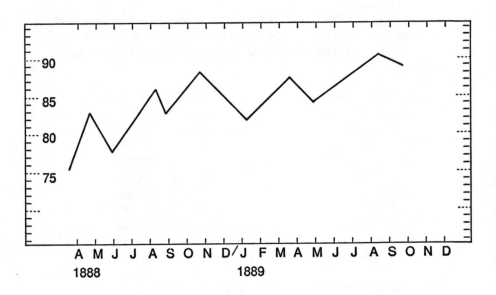

If this early list of average price movement, representing turning points, were placed on a line graph it would look like the figure above. It is readily observed that this is an early form of what is now called "technical analysis." These turning points actually represent areas of support and resistance. Two important factors in Dow Theory forecasting.

The list would be redesigned and refined many times in the following years. Charles Dow wanted to have more representation in the industrial stocks, as he likely realized they would eventually outperform the rails. At this time, however, there were not enough active industrial stocks to warrant a separate listing.

The Industrial and Railroad Average

Charles Dow reputedly kept elaborate charts of many different stocks for his personal and business use in investing. His investment firm of Goodbody, Glenn & Dow would have needed more intricate and detailed information than simple market averages.

This analysis and information eventually led Dow to include an Industrial Average in his newspaper. It also led Dow to notice the distinct "wavelike motions" which would become known later as The Dow Theory.

On May 26, 1896, the first Dow Industrial Average appeared as follows:

American Cotton Oil
American Sugar
American Tobacco
Chicago Gas
Distilling and Cattle Feeding
General Electric*
Laclede Gas
National Lead
North American
Tennessee Coal & Iron
U.S. Leather preferred
U.S. Rubber[4]

(*General Electric is the only company to appear with its original name on the current Dow Industrial list.)[5]

A few months later, in October of 1896, a revised Industrial Average and a Railroad Average both appeared in the *Journal*. This was an important milestone as the two averages would continue to be published from then to the present. The two averages would also provide the core of analysis for the Dow Theory of market moves and forecasting.

The two averages first appeared together as follows:

20 Railroad Average Stocks	12 Industrial Stocks
Erie	Am. Cotton Oil
Kansas & Texas pfd.	Am. Spirits Mfg.
Chesapeake & Ohio	Am. Sugar
Minneapolis & St. Ls 2d pfd.	Am. Tobacco
Susquehanna & Western pfd.	Chicago Gas
New York Central	General Electric
Atchinson	Laclede Gas
C.C.C. & St. Louis	National Lead
Southern R.R. pfd.	Tennessee Coal & In.
Missouri Pacific	U.S.Cordage pfd.
Jersey Central	U.S. Leather pfd.
Pacific Mail	U.S. Rubber
Northwest	
Louisville & Nashville	
Western Union	
Rock Island	
Burlington	
St. Paul	
Texas and Pacific	
Lakeshore[6]	

The daily movement of the Dow Averages also began to appear with the October 7, 1896, issue of the *Journal*. These averages would eventually become the main market indicators. The graph in Exhibit 2 depicts the daily price movement from Tuesday, September 8, through Tuesday, October 6, 1896.

The Industrial Average contained the stocks of companies that provided basic commodities, raw materials, and other necessities to life, commerce, and manufacturing. The products of these companies, such as gas, lead, and leather, were the building blocks of other developing industries. The companies born of these new industries would eventually become part of the Average as they grew and matured.

Exhibit 2 Early Dow Averages

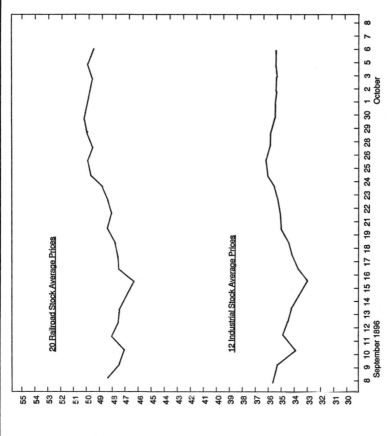

If the daily price averages had been placed on a line graph, they may have looked something like the figure above. Notice the tendency for the two averages to confirm each other.

The growing and maturing list of Industrials was changed many times in the early years, sometimes two or three times in the same year. In 1916, the list was increased to 20 stocks: the country was growing at a rapid pace and business finance was growing with it. As the economy moved through periods of fluctuation, for reasons often politically, militarily, or financially based, its varying signs of strength and weakness were reflected in the Dow.

On October 1, 1928, the number of stocks listed increased from 20 to 30. The new list contained 14 of the original 20, and 16 new companies. The list was changed for the same reason it has always changed: so that the average would be representative of the current stock market. Also in 1928, a special "divisor" was created to adjust the Dow Jones Averages for stock splits and stock dividends.

Averages as Indicators

Charles Dow firmly believed that the activity in the stock market was a reflection of all that was known about the financial health of the business economy. To Dow, the Railroad Average was the most important of all the indicators. The railroads, somewhat like the computer industry in the 1980s, were the fastest growing industry of the time.

As the predominant means of long distance transportation, railroads were important for many reasons. They not only shipped the raw materials to build and supply other industries, but when those industries had finished products, they would most often deliver them by rail. As the industries grew, and produced more finished goods to be shipped, so too did the railroads. Obviously, as they obtained more and more business, their earnings would also increase. This in turn meant more goods were being manufactured by the factories; therefore, the industrial earnings would also increase. In this way the railroads served as a leading indicator.

It was most likely this logic that led Charles Dow to create the two market averages. Another probable reason for two averages was the existence of manipulation of stocks. Two separate averages allowed more stocks to be listed and would make manipulation much more difficult. It was also realized, by Dow and others, that the industrial stocks would eventually outpace the railroads both in quantity and amount of business. Only so many railroads were needed, but industrial needs had an unlimited potential.

The Ever-changing Dow Averages

The Dow Jones Industrial Average, also known as "the Dow," "the Industrials" and "the Market," is a list of only 30 stocks which can provide endless delight or frustration to the investor. To many, the Dow is the same today as it was five or ten or twenty years ago. It is the same market their fathers or grandfathers lost money in during the Great Depression. To others, it is the Dow they made money in during the rally of 1986, and, to some, it is the same market they have been trying to outguess for the past two years. Today, that enigmatic list is composed of the following:

The 30 Dow Industrial Stocks 1/1/89

Allied Signal	Exxon	Phillip Morris
Alcoa	General Electric	Primerica
American Express	General Motors	Procter & Gamble
AT&T	Goodyear	Sears
Bethlehem Steel	IBM	Texaco
Boeing	Intl. Paper	USX Corp.
Chevron	McDonald's	Union Carbide
Coca-Cola	Merck	United Techs.
DuPont	3–M	Westinghouse
Eastman Kodak	Navistar	Woolworth

Investors and noninvestors alike make comparisons regarding the Dow. It's easy to do; discussion of the stock market makes some interesting conversation. It is fertile ground for differing opinions, and nearly everyone has some opinion of what might happen next.

It also makes interesting news, and newspapers and other media will often make comparisons.

Examples, such as "Another 1965 Style Rally," "Will the Dow Rally as in '86?" or "Another 1929 Crash?" can be found whenever the market is a hot topic of conversation. These types of headlines tend to reinforce comparisons of the Dow Industrial Average's current behavior to its colorful past. In the minds of many, the composition of the Dow Averages is as constant and unchanging as the surface of the moon. The facts, however, are quite different.

The Dow Averages are dynamic, not only in their movement, but also in their composition and structure. Through the years many changes have occurred. Some companies were removed, some new ones were added and the number of companies in the averages has changed. The companies themselves have also undergone changes.

Mergers have been a commonplace occurrence for many years. Occassionally a company is forced to divest itself of some of its holdings and is broken into smaller companies, as in recent years when the phone company was restructured.

As a result of this ever-changing nature, the Dow Averages of 1929, 1965, or even a year or two ago are separate and distinct entities. The overall complexion of 30 stocks in the Industrial Average and 20 in the Transportation Average is significantly altered by the removal and substitution of even one company. These changes, which are unavoidable, make comparisons of one year to another highly questionable.

The list of 30 Industrials has been modified several times since its creation (as 30 stocks) in 1928. After the crash of 1929 and the depression which followed, the list was changed more than twenty times. The earnings of large corporations were plummeting; as they fell lower in price, they were removed from the list. In 1929, the Dow reached a peak of 381.117 and by 1932 fell to a low of 41.22.

Change, in the economy and in business and, therefore, in the stock market, is inevitable. In 1988, we witnessed a resurgence of "merger mania," with companies such as R. J. Reynolds, Kraft and Pillsbury. For a while, it seemed as though the leveraged buyout was the only game in town. As companies are bought out, their stock stops trading and the money goes elsewhere. This is a form of condensing that can take place in the stock market.

It can be of value for the individual investor to know something of former cycles in the stock market, but it is also important to keep comparisons in perspective: the market indicators may have changed considerably in the time frame of the comparison.

The focus of comparison should always be on the current market situation. Looking back, perhaps as much as six months or one to two years may prove helpful in gaining perspective, but the most important question is, what is affecting the market now?

ENDNOTES

[1] Source: *Dow Jones Industrial Average,* by Richard J. Stillman, Published by Dow Jones-Irwin, 1986, p. 5.

[2] Ibid. pp. 12-14.

[3] Ibid. p. 14.

[4] Ibid. pp. 40, 41.

[5] Ibid. pp. 40, 41.

[6] Source: *Dow Industrial Average,* by Richard J. Stillman, published by Dow Jones-Irwin, 1986, p. 42. From an article appearing in *The Wall Street Journal,* October 7, 1896.

Chapter Four

A Condensed Market

A condensed market? All the talk over the past five years has been of an *expanded market*! The number of stocks available for trading is constantly increasing with new stock being issued or stock splits occurring. New companies are going public with initial public offerings (IPOs) every day. The time for trading activity is increasing. Only a couple of years ago an extra half hour was added to the trading day and there is talk of staying open for yet another half hour. The time increases are leading up to a twenty-four-hour stock market which could then lead to a coordinated *World Stock Market*, where an investor will be able to trade stocks on any exchange in the entire world, any time of the day or night. These are all important components of the expansion taking place in the stock market.

Yet, the stock market is also condensing in certain ways, and this can have an effect on how an investor plans strategies and places trades. Understanding the condensing effects in the market can indicate to the individual which market moves are significant, which moves indicate current sentiment, which moves indicate market apathy and which moves give warning signals of a weakening market.

The condensed market can be seen in the dramatic increase in trading volume over the past few years. The installation of computerized stock trading and clearing of stock trades has enabled the exchanges to trade hundreds of millions of shares each day with a great deal of ease. More shares are traded, with greater frequency and in a shorter period of time than ever would have been possible ten or twenty years ago. The increase in volume alone has an important condensing effect on the stock market.

Greater volume and frequency of trading also brings greater volatility. The sharp upward and downward swings of the stock market are occurring more often. There was a time when an increase in volatility was considered a bearish signal, but this is not necessarily the case anymore.

Causes of the Condensed Effect

Society, as a whole, is doing more and more in a shorter period of time. Many feel as if their lives are stuck in a kind of fast-forward mode. There are many causes for this phenomenon but the effect is the same: there is less and less time to accomplish more and more. The same is true of the stock market. Listed below are some of the causes of this condensing (fast forward) effect of the stock market.

New Investment Products

Brokerage firms base their very survival on the development and marketing of new types of investment products. Products which make investing easier, safer, and faster are coming to market every day. An early example of a new investment product was the advent of the mutual fund, which limited risk in the investing in any single company and made investing easier for both the large and small investor. A new version of the mutual fund, designed specifically for the institutional investor, is called the "basket investment." Like the mutual fund, it is sold as a product, but the differences are found primarily in the quantities of stock involved, as well as in the amount of dollars involved. A single basket unit may involve a couple hundred stocks and millions of dollars that can be repositioned in virtually a single transaction. There are other differences between the mutual fund and the basket of stocks, but their part in the condensing effect is quite similar.

Stock options have been with us for many years and have about the same impact as they always have had on the stock market. They can be highly speculative or defensive in nature. However, in the past few years index options and futures have come into being as new products. Their existence condenses the market with both increased volatility and changes in volume. Large traders will look closely to arbitrage situations existing between owning the actual stocks that make up the index, or in owning the options and futures on the index itself. Since options and futures have a time of expiration, the switching of cash from one investment product to the other can sharply affect the direction and volume of the market.

Mutual funds themselves are not really a new product, but there are new funds, new types of funds, and new investors coming along every day. The impact on the stock market is smaller initially as cash slowly comes into the fund, but can be quite pronounced as cash leaves the fund and the shares must be redeemed (converted to cash).

The upward price pressure of a mutual fund may continue over an extended period of years. As the funds grow to billions of dollars' worth of stock, they help the value of these stocks increase and the market rises. If, however, they must suddenly liquidate their positions in order to meet their redemptions, the results can be devastating to the stock market. This was one of the complicating situations which existed in the severe market drop in October of 1987.

The individual investor can participate in an investment product that is similar in makeup to the "basket" approach. This product has been around for a few years, but has become more prevalent in the last couple of years. It is the closed-end mutual fund. The closed-end fund has a definite number of shares and trades on the stock exchanges, just like regular listed stocks. One share of the closed-end fund may represent portions of shares of several hundred different companies. The value of these shares like individual stocks, will fluctuate depending on whether there are more buyers or sellers, but is not necessarily directly related to the intrinsic value of the stocks contained. In fact it is quite common for closed-end funds to trade at a discount to (less than) their intrinsic, or net asset value.

These funds have effectively removed these stocks from trading and instead trade an artificial security which represents the stocks contained therein. The combined effect of these funds is the isolation of their stocks, thereby increasing market volatility.

Rapid News Information

The news media of today prides itself in being able to report the news information "as it happens." In reality, of course, this is not possible, although the news is being reported with increasing speed around the world. Communications satellites, microwave transmissions, cable networks, and other electronic marvels have hastened the reporting of news developments considerably as compared to earlier years.

An earthquake in Armenia was reported around the world in a matter of minutes after it occurred. A severe frost on the orange groves in Florida is known the following day when trading in commodities opens. News of an important corporate takeover can be known by all within minutes of the initial announcement. Today it takes minutes, 10 years ago it took hours and 20 years ago it may have taken a couple of days. A hundred years ago the news could have taken weeks to reach the interested public.

Taking a few weeks for news of important economic events to reach the public made it difficult for investors during the days of Charles Dow. He made the recommendation to "the out of town trader" to make use of "stop orders" to protect investments in the stock market. This can still be a good strategy for any investor who is not able to closely monitor the stock market.

During the trading day, the most instantaneous news comes from the wire services. Institutional traders keep a constant eye on the news developments which are being transmitted on their large screen monitors. Individual investors can also subscribe to a news wire service (see Chapter Fourteen).

Instant news means the investor can react swiftly to economic developments. Transactions which formerly may have taken a day to two to be completed can be analyzed and initiated within minutes.

If the news is in a condensed time period as compared to earlier days, then it also has a condensing effect on the stocks being traded in the market.

Market Information Monitoring

The institutional investor also has another source of information available to make investment decisions. That is the constant monitoring of movements in the stock market as well as other events that influence the market.

Access to the market averages, the bond market (which tells what interest rates are doing, based on the current price of bonds), the strength of the dollar, the trend of gold and other precious metals' prices, the current rise or fall in oil and other related information gives the institutional investor an edge in implementing trading strategies. This access also has the effect of condensing the market activity for reasons similar to being able to react more quickly to news items.

As this market analysis information becomes more available to the individual investor, the condensing of market activity will be even more greatly accelerated.

Computer Trading

The computer, that wonderful development which can store and compare information more accurately and completely than the best of human minds, works in various ways in trading.

The computer analyzes moves in the stock market to give buy and sell signals. This enables the large stock trader to act effectively in implementing strategy.

Also, the computer can be actively involved in placing buy and sell orders based on the program input, (programmed trading). The instantaneous nature of this can only further condense the activity in the stock market.

It should be noted that computerized trading (programmed trading) is not always profitable and is not always in effect. As with any trading system, there are too many variables affecting the market, including the presence of the computerized trading itself, which can cause the stock market to give out many false signals as to market direction.

Evidence

The evidence of a condensing market can be seen in different areas. Some of the strongest evidence appears in the increase in trading volume over the past few years.

Just a quick glance at the chart in Exhibit 1 clearly illustrates how condensed the amount of trading has become.

Evidence can also be seen of the increase in stock market volatility over the past few years. The amazingly quick recovery from a severe drop in the stock market and, of course, the amazing speed with which the market can drop are easily observed.

Further evidence can be found in the fact that the basic concept of the Dow Theory can be observed in the trading that occurs within a day. See Exhibit 2.

The Effects

Trading frequently on the concept of the stock market being condensed (in terms of activity) means the investor needs to be aware of certain effects this condensing can have.

Charles Dow, William Hamilton, and others talked of bull and bear markets in terms of four to six years. Now they must be thought of in considerably shorter time periods. Stock market cycles which once took days, weeks, or months can now occur in minutes or hours; this is particularly true of secondary reactions. A secondary reaction may move so quickly that it is totally recovered in a couple of days or less.

The problem is further complicated by the fact that the market can proceed at different speeds. One week it may be slow and lethargic and the next week it may shift into a fast-forward mode. This ability to apparently change speeds has made things difficult for the analyst who likes to study market momentum. Not being aware of these rapid changes can place the investor on the wrong side of the market.

The trader of stock can no longer rely solely on closing statistics to plan and implement trading strategies. Because the stock market activity has become condensed, the movement of the market in motion is as important as the level at which it closes. Did the market reach an intra-day peak and begin to retreat? Or, did a strong rally

Exhibit 1   Volume Increase

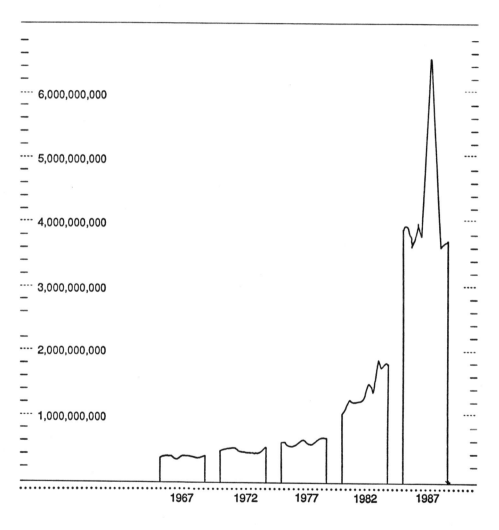

Graph shows the monthly trading volume on the New York Stock Exchange. Volume in number of shares traded.

Exhibit 2 Volatility

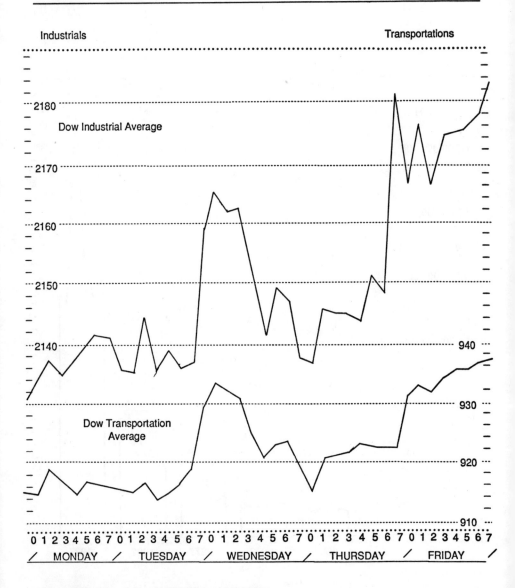

Hourly Trading: from 10/17/88 to 10/21/88.
Notice the trend confirmation and lack of confirmation.

begin in the last couple of hours of trading, a rally which is likely to continue into the next trading day? This information is especially useful when using the market averages and other indicators.

Chapter Five

Market at Rest—In Motion

The fact is, it's all history. Many investors forget this all-important fact when they are planning their strategy or placing their orders. Any information regarding the stock market is essentially historical information which may or may not illuminate coming events. Not only is the information historical, but also it has likely been seen by millions of people by the time the individual investor becomes informed.

So, to which history is the investor going to look? From the beginning of existence to the present? The past five years or the past six months? Or, should an investor look at immediate history of the past few days, hours or minutes?

The easy answer is that it depends on how much time an individual has to study historical data. It can be helpful to analyze the course of an individual stock, but only in the way in which it relates to present information.

It is the present situation which determines the value of one particular company over another. What's happening now, is the question an investor should always be asking. Although a positive future outlook is also important, what's happening now is more important than what happened a month ago, or a year ago. This is true of individual stocks and the whole market.

Information of the stock market exists in two different forms, although most people only consider one. The market at rest is based on closing prices, and the market in motion is based on prices moving throughout the day. Most investors only consider the closing statistics in their trading strategy, even though they must place their trades while the market is in motion. This can lead to some unpleasant surprises, as they may receive what is often called a "bad fill."

For example, an investor places a sell order for 500 shares of AT&T when the last trade showing was 27. The 500 shares sell at a price of 26 1/4 and the stock closes for the day at 29. Although this situation can occur at any time, a look at the market in motion can help to avoid unpleasant surprises and fill your stock order where you anticipated it to be filled.

As many investors know, stocks tend to move as a group, particularly the stocks traded on the major exchanges. This very fact can be of some assistance in placing orders, if you have some idea of what to look for in evaluating the situation. If stocks move as a group, it can be valid to look at the direction of the market leaders.

The Dow Jones Industrial Average and Transportation Average are two groups of large companies which tend to lead the market. Exhibit 1 shows both averages over a one-week period of time. The chart in Exhibit 1 tracks two sets of price levels, or, more accurately, point levels of times in which the market would have been at rest.

It can be seen that the Dow tended to close on the upside through Thursday, with a bit of a correction on Friday, which left it down a few points for the week. Looked at from a stock trader's view, Thursday would have been a good day to sell and Friday the best day to buy.

Notice the tendency of the Transportation Average to track the Dow Industrials. This is important. It is an integral part of the Dow Theory, which is still very much used by regular stock traders, both at the institutional and individual investor levels. The two averages will confirm each other in their trend movements. Therefore, it is important to notice this "confirmation," and any possible divergence. Note the Transportation Average was actually up a small amount for the week. Note also, that this is a picture of the market at rest.

Observing closing levels of the market can be somewhat helpful in determining the primary and secondary trends of the stock

Exhibit 1 Market at Rest

At the Market Open and At the Market Close Levels of Industrials and Transports

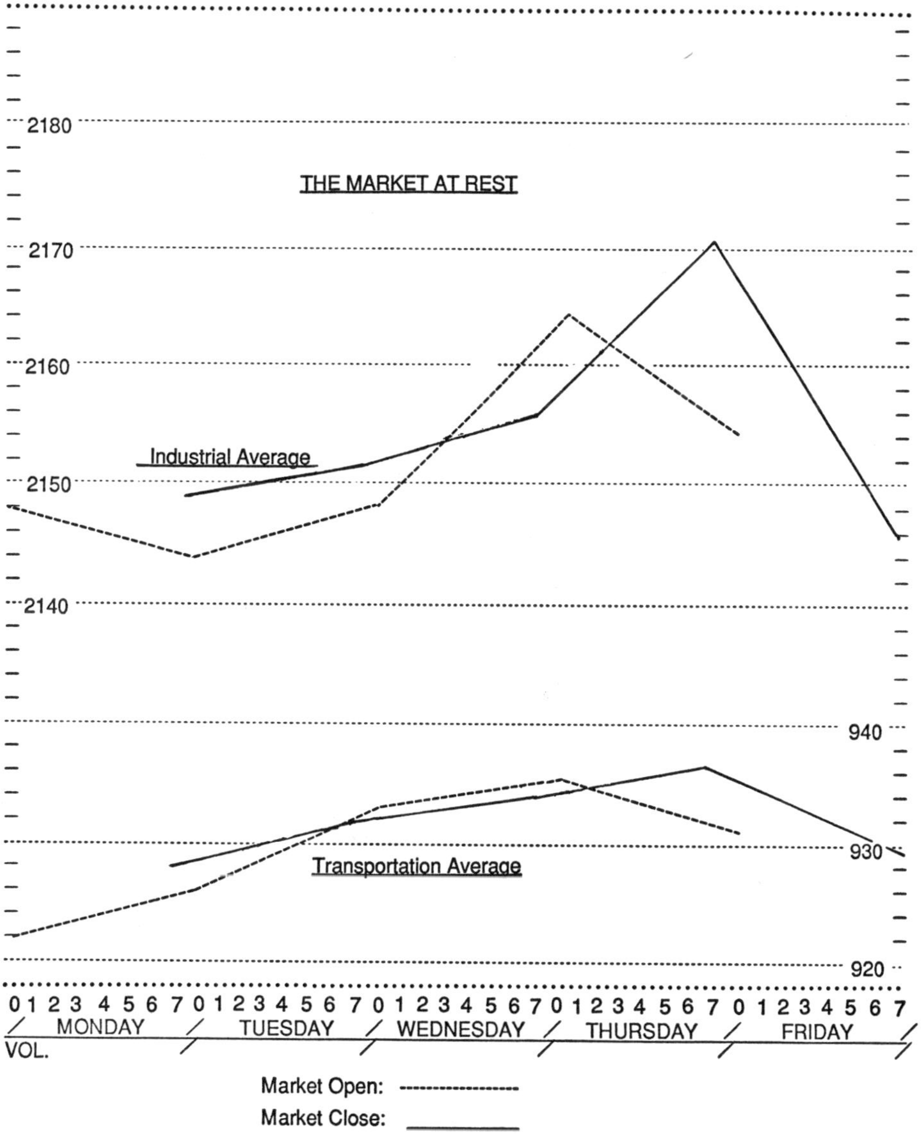
2180
THE MARKET AT REST
2170
2160
Industrial Average
2150
2140
940
930
Transportation Average
920
0 1 2 3 4 5 6 7 0 1 2 3 4 5 6 7 0 1 2 3 4 5 6 7 0 1 2 3 4 5 6 7 0 1 2 3 4 5 6 7
MONDAY
TUESDAY
WEDNESDAY
THURSDAY
FRIDAY
VOL.
Market Open:
Market Close:

market. It may be compared to watching the win/loss record of a favorite baseball team. You may not have time to watch all of the games, but you do want to know how the game ended as it has an effect on their standing in the league. However, once a baseball game is over, it's over, never to be played again.

The stock market is quite different. It plays the same game every single trading day. As long as a stock is trading, there is no such thing as the game being over. Therefore, it is important to have some knowledge and understanding of what the market is doing as it moves. This is especially true when placing a buy or sell transaction.

Take another look at the same week of trading in the Dow Industrials and Transports. This time look at the hourly movement of the two averages as shown in Exhibit 2. Two facts will become quite obvious. First, there was a great deal of action during the days involved and second, the instances of divergence between the two averages is more apparent. Particularly, note the Transportation Average through Tuesday, Wednesday and Thursday. It appears to be moving up rather steadily, while the Dow appears to bob and weave, not knowing whether to advance or decline. Looked at from the point of placing buy or sell orders, it is easy to see the different results possible, depending on when the orders were placed. Friday may have been a good day to buy, but not necessarily at the third trading hour. Monday may have been an even better day.

Thursday still looks like the best sell day, but not until about an hour before the market closed. Notice the drop in the Dow Industrials on Wednesday, but a correspondingly minor drop in the Transportation Average. This appears to "slingshot" the Dow to the high for the week.

Also notice the daily volume figures, these are the end of the day volume figures. Used here they illustrate a couple of points. 1988 had been a rather light trading year as far as volume was concerned. Stock trading had been cautious due to a change in tax laws, the economic conditions and the severe market correction in October of the previous year. Trading volume tended to run between 100 million and 200 million shares per day. Notice that on Wednesday and Thursday, when the market was in a rally, the

Exhibit 2 Market in Motion

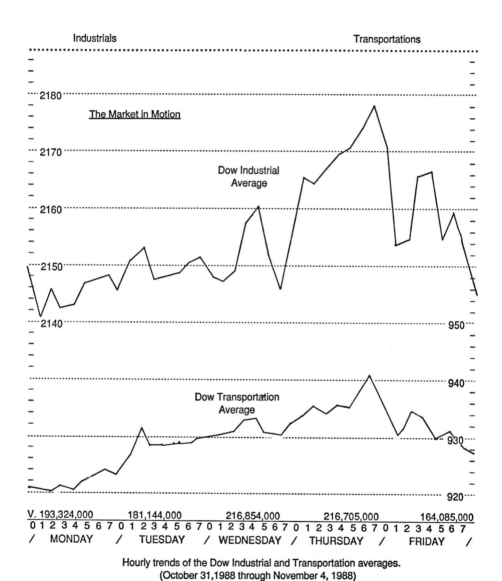

Hourly trends of the Dow Industrial and Transportation averages.
(October 31,1988 through November 4, 1988)

volume tended to be on the heavy side. When the correction came on Friday, the volume was considerably lighter. This tendency is important to notice because it strongly suggests the existence of a bull market. Again, this is a concept of The Dow Theory: stronger volume on market rallies and weaker volume on market corrections are signs of strong bullish sentiment in the market.

To say that the stock market will predict future trends is a matter of continual hot debate. However, looking at the information on the hourly chart in Exhibit 2, one can easily see that a Thursday rally was strongly indicated for several reasons.

- The upward trend for the week.
- The increase in volume on Wednesday.
- The drop and recovery on Wednesday.
- The steady upward progress of the Transportation Average.

Whether placing trades for short- or long-term trading, consideration of the market in motion can be even more important than looking only at the market at rest.

Chapter Six

What Are the
"Heavy Hitters" Doing?

S tock market speculators have been active from the early days of stock trading. Individual investors have always attempted to "ride on the coat tails" of the expert traders. Sometimes they are manipulated; other times they have made a profit in the process.

In the early days of the market, there were many colorful names and exploits in market speculations. Andrew Craigie of Boston, the former apothecary general of the Continental Army, became a funnel of foreign funds into American securities and was "well known" for his activities. The infamous William Duer, purported to be the first major stock speculator (or major scoundrel), did rather well in land speculation, but got carried away on bank stock speculation as well as manipulation. He also became the first major stock market victim in the crash of 1792.

In the 1860s, Daniel Drew, the creator of "watered stock" and his personal money machine, the Erie Railroad, became well known for his battles with "Commodore" Cornelius Vanderbilt. The Commodore's actions in the stock market were said to cause "ripples of activity on the street." These were the early "movers and shakers," the "heavy hitters," and the "experts" of Wall Street.

Today, in the 1980s, the names are different, but the activities are similar. Consider for instance, Carl Icahn, famous for his airline and other activities, T. Boone Pickens, with his oil company action, or Ross Perot, the computer time big operator.

Their actions, like their predecessors', have an impact on the entire market, even though their targets are generally limited to specific companies. It is advisable for the individual investor to be aware of the actions of these and other large money speculators. This includes the deal makers, but also another large important group, the institutional investors.

"Pools" of money have existed since the early days, when funds from Europe flowed to this new "land of opportunity." The French, the Dutch, and others were quick to recognize the ground floor opportunity of business created by this new country. Even today, foreign funds will flow into the U.S. markets when the market is bullish. The most influential "pools" now are in different hands than they were in the early days.

The "institutional investors," are now the pools. They are composed of insurance companies, mutual funds, pension funds, or large corporations controlled by investment advisors. The investment advisors may work directly for a particular institution, or may be an independent company set up on a consulting basis.

The institutional analysts and traders are well educated in areas of economics, finance, and the action of the stock market. They are well aware of the Dow Theory, technical analysis, and probably a dozen or more other theories on the stock market.

These lions of Wall Street are experienced at reading the indicators to determine which way the market will go next. They are the "experts" of what is happening in the stock market. At times they are actually the cause of what the market is doing. If an individual has some idea of what the experts are doing, the information may prove valuable in planning strategy.

The institutional traders can play with the market in an attempt to get some action going. They can "kick out the stops" on a stock with a strong selling program, pulling other institutional sellers into their wake. When the price collapses to a low enough level, the traders can initiate buying programs which bring the stock back up to its former level and above.

Note that "kicking out the stops" refers to selling a stock with sufficient quantity to activate stop loss orders which are placed under the current market price. The traders cannot know where these stop orders are, but they are usually within 10 percent of the current stable or average price. As the stop orders are activated, the price may drop a dollar or more just from the momentum of these automatic sells.

At times an institution may feel abused or bored with the current market and pull the assets to the sideline. They may place their funds into money market investments or fixed income bonds and wait for opportunity to again appear.

Opportunity can be elusive at times, waiting in the shadows of a slow, lethargic market. Opportunity may suddenly appear in the form of a positive economic announcement, or possibly a rumor, or unexpected upswing. It may actually be created by a "fishing expedition" with some programmed buying to see if anyone else is interested. Since all of the players are watching the market all of the time, they can crank up their computers to get in on the action.

Suddenly, we have a storming rally. Volume sharply increases, the Dow Industrial Average surges upward, with the Transportation Average in tow. Gradually, the broad market joins in the rally and away we go toward new highs.

Somewhere in the flurry of this excited crowd, one or more of the players decides to begin taking profits. The upward surge begins to thin and weaken, as shown by the advance/decline line narrowing, or a drop in overall volume. The market may even be seen to stumble a bit, not quite able to break through the high of yesterday or this morning. The market can then suddenly turn direction and head south looking for a new support level. At first it may slowly drift downward with some hesitancy; this can quickly become an unglorious retreat.

Then, selling programs come into effect. The cumulative tick may be a minus 400 or 600 or more. The trin may register 3.0 or higher. Prices fall to recent levels and below. No one wants to be left holding the bag, and the bag is becoming worth less and less. If the prices fall far enough, but not too far, opportunity again makes its presence known and the buying begins again.

The intentional manipulation of stock prices is an illegal activity, however it is legal to buy stock and to sell that stock if it does not perform as expected. This is a difficult legal point both in definition and enforcement. When is it manipulation and when is it a legal investment strategy? Because influence on price swings is difficult to define and control, it does exist, adding to the natural volatility of the stock market.

Rally and correction cycles may occur in a few hours, a few days or a few weeks or longer. At times they may be initiated by the large traders. At other times these cycles are just a normal progression of the stock market. If an individual investor is to trade frequently, it is important to understand some of the factors involved and how to read the signs.

The longer term investment strategies of institutional investors can be learned from the financial newspapers, magazines, and newsletters. These sources of information will discuss current strategies and the conditions affecting them. The new trend of creating "packaged products" or "baskets" of stocks, and how this approach is likely to affect the stock market, is one example of these new strategies.

Another topic of frequent debate is the disappearance of "value investing" caused by the switching from stocks to stock futures, or index options, and back again. This is a strategy commonly used by the large institutional stock market traders. The value of a particular stock is not considered in this strategy, it is another form of arbitrage trading.

Not only is it important to be aware of what the "heavy hitters" are up to in their strategy, but an investor must also be aware of the action of the "big guys" when placing an order. The question must be "what are they doing *now*?" This can be learned by tracking the beast.

Chapter Seven

Tracking the Beast: Technical Points

Experienced wilderness guides and expert trackers claim that the art of following a creature is not quite as simple as following a set of footprints. If it were that easy, anyone with adequate eyesight could do the same. Expert tracking involves reading signs when they are available; it also requires deduction, logic and a certain ability to match wits with the creature of pursuit.

Ideally, tracking is the ability to outguess the next move of the beast and be present at the arrival of the prey.

Market tracking or "technical analysis" is the record and study of where the market has been in the hope of predicting where it will go next. Economic or fundamental analysis of stocks or the market is considered to be of little importance. The market movement is the focus of attention. The basic philosophy behind technical analysis is the belief in certain mathematical unities that are pervasive throughout existence. "Technical analysis" is used with the market in general, as well as individual stocks.

In the early 1900s, Charles Dow referred to "watching the tide." He was comparing the movement of the stock market to the tide washing up on the sand.[1]

Dow was also referring to his Industrial Average and Transportation Average (then called the Railroad Average), which first appeared in *The Wall Street Journal*, in 1889, the *Journal's* first publication.

In his comparison, Charles Dow asks the reader to imagine a sandy beach with the waves washing up on the shore. If a stick is placed into the sand at the high point of a wave, the observer can tell if the tide is coming in or going out.

The stock market, when observed from fixed points, can display a similar action. When new highs are not being achieved, the market may be receding to lower levels. As former highs are penetrated, the market may rise to yet other new highs. These are the "tracks" of the market.

Although it takes a little stretch of the imagination, this does appear to resemble the tides washing up on the beach. (See Exhibit 1.) The stick would be placed in the sand by point B, the highest point for this time period. The letters are placed at points of "resistance." These are points where the Dow Industrials failed to go higher and reversed direction. The numbers are placed at points of "support." In effect, support is the opposite of resistance: it is the level where buyers come on to the scene and the market stops falling.

Note the first three days when the market rallied to point A, ran into resistance at the 2160 level, and pulled back to a somewhat weaker (lower) support level. From that support a strong rally ensued, carrying the Dow through the 2160 resistance 20 points higher to the 2180 resistance level. At this level, the rally weakened as it moved to point B. Obviously the weakening caused concern. The market fell to support at the 2170 level; some might call this a "trial support level." The weak rally to point C said to many investors that it was time to pull out and start selling. The market then pulled back to the next support level at number 4. This was a fairly strong support level as the market had been supported near the 2140 level three times in less than ten days. The nearly ten-point rally on the eleventh day looks rather like a trial rally, just there to see if anybody is interested.

The resistance encountered at the 2150 level is reinforced by first having broken through on a downswing and then turning the market back at point D. The hesitancy can be seen as the market cautiously moves to point E and rather slowly crawls through the 2150 resistance-level. Notice the much steeper angle as it moves farther up from the resistence level. Obviously, there is strong resistance at the 2170 level. Once the turn occurred at this level all bets

Exhibit 1 Technical Points

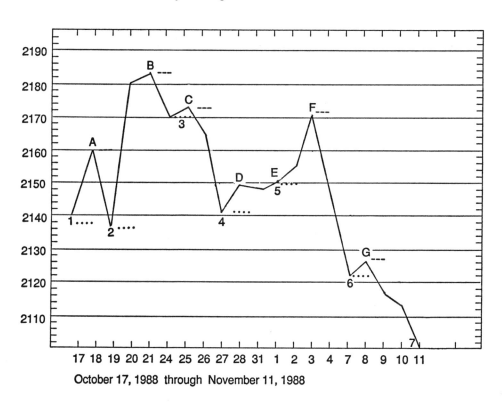

Daily Closing Prices: Dow Industrials

October 17, 1988 through November 11, 1988

In his comparison, Charles Dow asks the reader to Imagine a sandy beach with the waves washing up on the shore. If a stick is placed into the sand at the high point of a wave, watching will tell the observer if the tide is coming in or receding. The stock market, when observed from fixed points can display a similar action. When new highs are not being achieved, the market may be receding to lower levels. As former highs are penetrated, the market may rise to yet other new highs. These are the "tracks" of the market.

were off; this was the fourth time in a few days. Again it was time to look for a new support-level and the market fell.

The Dow didn't even slow down for the 2140 level of former support (remember it was a strong support level), but dropped to the 2125 area as a new trial. A weak buying session quickly said it was time to go further south and that is what the market did.

Charles Dow might have interpreted this chart something like this: The turning point at A is of concern, until we see the strong penetration to point B. The pullback to point C isn't of much concern unless it is followed by another surge which fails to penetrate either point C or point B. Since point F illustrates this failure, the market is most certain to seek lower levels.

Even though these movements are tertiary in nature (being only a period of 20 days), they may represent a significant secondary reaction in a slow primary bull market.

Dow was concerned more with the points of resistance, and the continued failure to break through, than he was with the support levels.

These are the "tracks of the beast." The beast is the combined impact of those bulls or bears who most strongly affect the market. Although they do not control the market, these investors make measurable moves which can be observed. The actual moves are often best observed looking at short terms of hourly or daily duration. Tracking the beast can give the investor somewhat of a feeling of the strength, intensity, and direction of the market. The main focus should always be the longer term primary trend, but attention to the shorter term trend can also be helpful. After all, the turn of the primary trend will occur in the short-term action. In addition to this, it is important to remember that orders to buy or sell stock are placed in an active short-term market.

In looking at Exhibit 1, if one had placed an order to buy a Dow Industrial type of stock on the third day and followed the progress, one may have been ready to sell in the rally from E to F and been able to wait calmly for the next strong support level. These are the profits from trading which can be quite pleasing.

It is important to be aware of the technical factors of resistance and support whether the view is short term or longer. Thus far these factors have been observed over a four-week period of time with the stock market at rest. As was discussed in the chapter on the Market in Motion, the picture may become even more clear from the dynamic view.

Exhibits 2–5 will look at the same four weeks; however, these graphs will look at the market in motion on an hourly basis. Also included are the hourly movement graphs of the Dow Transportation Average. Notice the existence of the coinciding movement between the two averages as well as some interesting areas of divergence. Some of these periods of divergence appear to be predictive and some do not.

Divergence between the Dow Industrials and the Dow Transports will not usually last for a long period of time. There appears to be a natural tendency for the two averages to track each other and an arbitrage situation is often created by the divergence. This can mean quick profits for the large trader. Stock traders know that the two averages will line up and they place trades in anticipation of the event.

Support and resistance are but two of the most basic elements of technical analysis. There have been many books published on the study of this special science. The full study can be quite involved and take a great deal of time to learn. Understanding the simple concepts of support and resistence can help the individual investor to understand market moves and place more effective stock transactions when buying and selling. Support and resistance can also be effective in timing the buying and selling of individual stocks.

ENDNOTES

[1] Source: *The Wall Street Journal,* January 31, 1901, p. 1.

Exhibit 2 Hourly Tracking 10/17–21, 1988

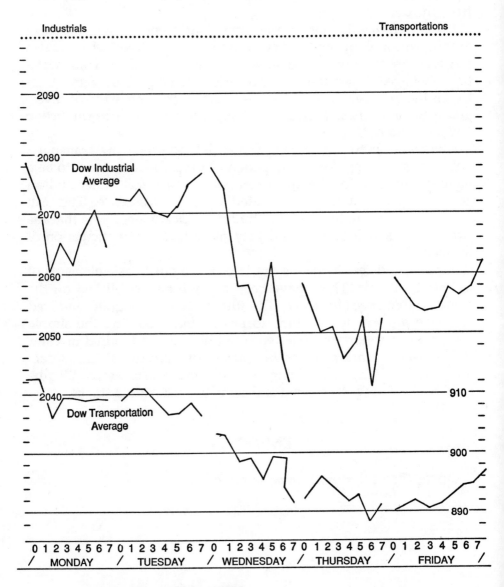

Hourly Tracking: 10/17/88 to 10/21/88

Exhibit 3 Hourly Tracking 10/24–28, 1988

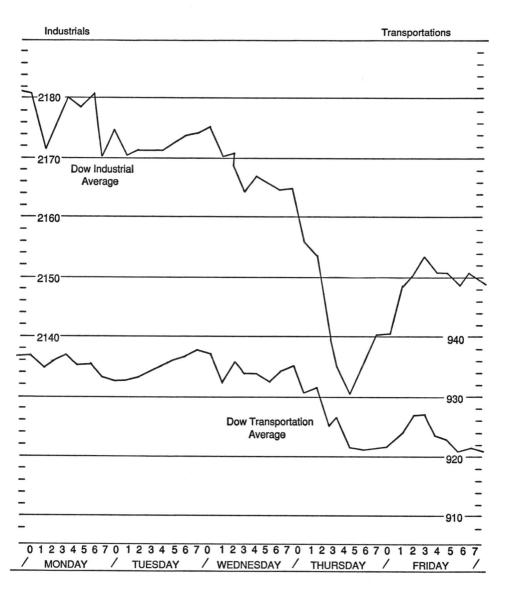

Hourly Tracking: 10/24/88 through 10/28/88.

Exhibit 4 Hourly Tracking 10/31–11/4, 1988

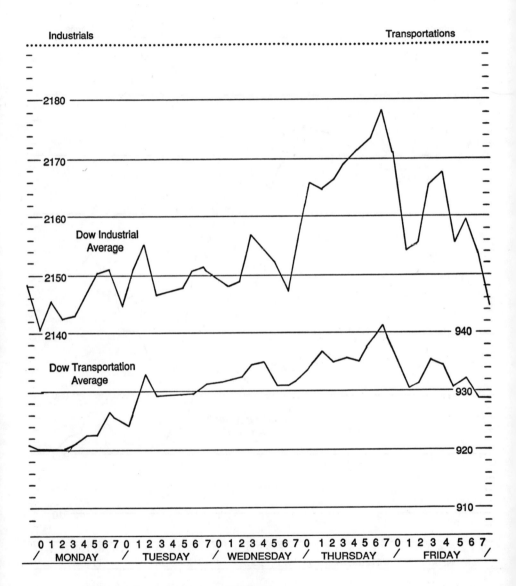

Hourly Tracking: 10/24/88 through 10/28/88.

Exhibit 5 Hourly Tracking 11/7–11, 1988

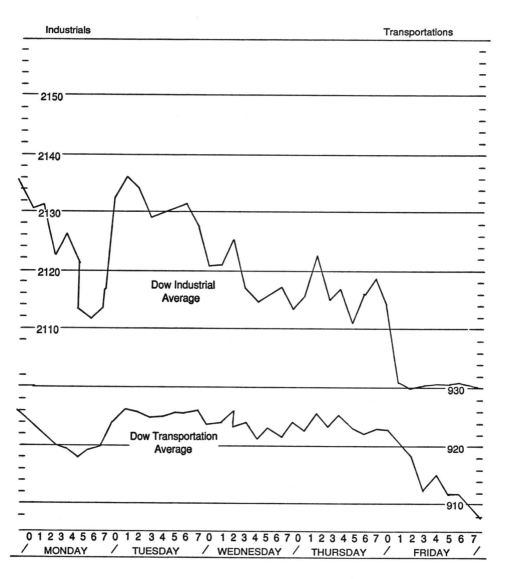

Hourly Tracking: from 11/7/88 to 11/11/88

Chapter Eight

Market Indicators

Market indicators tell an investor where the market has been, where it is currently, and where it may be going in the future. Just as the ancients would consult with oracles, seers, and prophets to know what might happen next, modern investors will consult the stock market indicators.

There is no set formula for choosing a particular type or number of market indicators to follow. This depends on the amount of time and interest which an individual has to devote to tracking and analysis. Professional stock traders may follow as many as eighty or more indicators. Some individuals may follow only one indicator. There are hundreds of indicators to choose from; some are economic, others are technical and some are literally "out of this world." There are some analysts who are reported to base investment advice on the alignment of the planets.

First is a look at the active indicators. Those indicators which can be tracked on an hourly and daily basis. They might also be called technical indicators, as they involve the market movements rather than value fundamentals of the underlying securities.

The following is a list of the active market indicators. They are indicators which can be easily followed, whether in talking to a broker as a trade is placed or checking a financial newspaper for the statistics. They can also be easily followed by those who use a computer for investing.

Stock market indicators:

- The Dow Industrial Average
- The Dow Transportation Average
- The Dow Utility Average
- Market Volume
- New Highs and New Lows
- Moving Averages
- S & P 500

The Dow Industrial Average

The Dow Industrial Average is a list of 30 "industrial" stocks whose prices are averaged and indexed to stock splits and additions. The average is quoted in terms of points and is available at any time during the trading day or in the newspaper on the following day. Financial newspapers will generally quote the opening, hourly, and closing levels.

The Dow Industrial Average is considered by many to actually be the stock market. Since it is composed of the largest capitalization companies which also tend to be the most frequently traded stocks, the Industrial Average does tend to point the main direction of the current market. There are times when the Industrials and the rest of the market are not going in the same direction, but this is fairly rare and can signal a turning point.

The Dow Transportation Average

The Dow Transportation Average is composed of 20 stocks which are a part of the commercial transportation industry. Basically, it is comprised of railroad, trucking, and airlines companies. The average is calculated and reported in much the same way as the Industrial Average. It has also gone through similar changes throughout the years. The major change was in 1970 when the list was changed from the "Railroad Average" to the "Transportation Average." The following is the current listing of the Dow Transportation Average companies.

The Dow Transportation Average

AMR Corp	Delta Air	SowestAir
Amer. Pres	Federal Exp.	Tiger Int'l.
Burlington	NWA	UAL Corp.
CSX	NorfolkSo	Union Pac
CarolnFt	Pan Am Cp	US Air
ConsldFt	Ryder Sys	XtraCp
ConsldRl	SantaFSP	

The Transportation Average can be useful in two main ways:

- As a confirming indicator of the direction of the Dow Industrial Average.

- As a sector indicator for stocks involved with commercial transportation.

As the Industrial Average moves up, down or remains unchanged, the Transportation Average will track the movement proportionately. This is called the confirmation of the trend.

At times, a divergence will occur between the two averages. The Industrial Average may be up twenty points from the previous day, while the Transportation Average is down a point or unchanged. When a divergence such as this occurs, an adjustment will soon be made. Either the rally in the Industrial Average will turn and begin to drop, or the Transportation Average will start to rally until it again comes more in line with the leader.

Although one can never tell for certain which adjustment will be made to a divergence, tracking the two averages will indicate the current pattern of adjustment. For example, if transports have adjusted upward to be in line with the Industrials after a divergence occurs, and this has been happening for the past few months, there is a likelihood that this upward adjustment will occur again.

The previous examples assume that other indicators remain on the bullish side. Is the total market volume strong and bullish, is the advance/decline line bullish, are there buying programs in effect, does the trin indicate a current buying status? Checking other indicators can at least increase the chances of understanding the next market adjustment.

The Transportation Average used as an industry sector indicator can tell the investor if a trend of an individual stock is unique or is a result of an event which is having an impact on the entire transportation industry. For example, if an investor is holding stock of a trucking company not found in the Dow Transportation Average, and the stock is advancing while the Average is declining, there is most likely positive news on the company. If this divergence continues, and the Transportation Average continues to decline, the individual stock will begin to decline also, even with positive news. This can be a time to take some protective action in order to preserve profits. Either sell the stock, place a "stop" order, or consider a defensive option strategy.

Whether the Transportation Average is used as a confirming indicator or a sector indicator it can be a valuable indicator for the individual investor to watch. It may bring more questions than answers at times, but finding the answers to questions raised can improve the effectiveness of an investment strategy.

The Dow Utility Average

The Utility Average can also be called the "overlooked" indicator. If an investor walks into a stock brokerage office and is able to listen to the brokers answering questions for their clients, giving stock quotes, and telling them where the Dow is currently heading, that investor would seldom hear the Utility Average being quoted. In fact, if the Utility Average is being checked, it is usually because the person doing the asking is holding utility stock.

If an investor spends time each day reading *The Wall Street Journal*, *Investor's Daily*, or other financial newspapers, the time is generally spent reading the news briefs, the stock or option quotes and maybe some of the fun or interesting articles. Only a select few will even glance at the current trend of interest rates, or the trend of the Utility Average.

The list on the following page is the list of the fifteen Utility Average stocks in 1989.

Am. Elec. Power	Cons Nat Gas	Panhandl E
Center. Energy	Detroit Edison	Peoples En
Columbia Gas	Houston Ind.	Phila. Elec.
Commonwealth Ed.	Niagra Mohwk.P	PSE
Consol Edison	Pacific G&E	SCE Corp.

The Dow Utility Average is a mirror of interest rates. Utility stock is a kind of hybrid between a stock and a bond; therefore, it tends to be less volatile in the short-term movement. The importance of the Utility Average as an indicator of the direction of current interest rates is explained in the following:

> Dow Jones Utility Average: Because of their sensitivity to interest rates, the utility stocks are often seen as a bellwether for the entire market. Utility stocks are more sensitive to interest rates than other stocks for two reasons: 1) utilities are heavy borrowers and thus their earnings are easily hurt by rising interest rates; and 2) utilities customarily pay a high dividend yield and are often purchased as a substitute for bonds. When interest rates rise, investors are likely to sell their utility stocks—purchased originally for their yield— and rush to higher yielding short-term instruments such as T-bills. Thus, the Dow Jones Utility Average is often considered to be a leading indicator for the major trend of the stock market.[1]

While these are good reasons to keep an eye on the Dow Jones Utility Average, it is also important to keep in mind that there are other factors affecting the Utility Average. Weather, for example, has a direct influence on electrical power usage and, consequently, affects the earnings and profits of certain utilities.

It could be said that the Utility Average foreshadowed the drop in the Dow Industrials in October of 1987. The Utility Average began giving signals as early as April of 1987, when it dropped below its 200-day moving average. Utilities stayed below that 200-day average until mid-August when they made a small effort at a breakthrough. Unable to maintain an upward trend, utilities again fell below the 200-day average and stayed there through the end of the year.

This indicated the strength of rising interest rates. The stock market and interest rates cannot continue to climb together for an extended period of time. Eventually one or the other will become dominant. In 1987, as we well know, it was the rising interest rates which eventually prevailed.

The Utility Average can also be used as another confirming factor of the current market trend. Consider the following description:

> ...another average that can be used in this regard, the Dow Utility Average. Because the DJU represents a sector of the market peculiarly influenced by such factors as money rates and industrial activity, it is a technically useful barometer, even for those who are such swingers that they'd never buy a staid utility stock. Many times the DJU has led the rest of the market, topping out and heading down (or bottoming out and heading up) before the DJI.

This almost sounds as though it was written as a description of the crash of 1987, but in fact it was written many years prior to that event. The similarity grows even greater:

> When this average, which usually leads the rest, refuses to participate in a rally, not just for one or two days, but for a couple of weeks or more, it is a warning of potential trouble for the rest of the list. Once again, divergence is the signifier.[2]

Exhibit 1 shows the Dow Utility Average in an eight-week period from November 18, 1988, through January 13, 1989. It is immediately apparent that the utility average is not as volatile nor as extreme as either the Dow Industrials or the Transportation Average. This tendency for low volatility is also readily observed in the hourly tracking, when the market is in motion.

It is interesting to notice the rise of the Utility Average on the eight-week graph. This was a time period when short-term interest rates were rising; one would expect the utility stocks to be falling in price. There were two main reasons for the phenomena:

- The Average was pushed up by four extraordinarily active stocks. (Detroit Edison, Peoples Energy, Panhandle Eastern, and Commonwealth Edison had more than a 20 percent gain for 1988. The total gain on the Utility Average was just over 6 percent.)

Exhibit 1   Dow Jones Utility Average

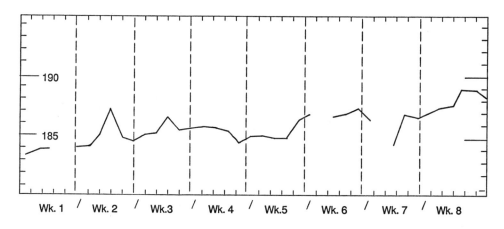

Daily Closes: 11/18/88 through 1/13/89

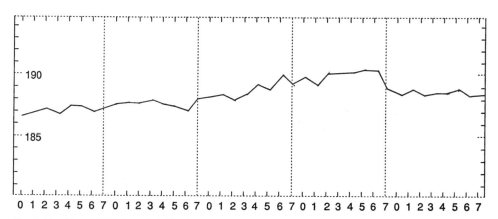

Hourly Tracking: 1/9/89 through 1/13/89

- The long-term interest rates remained low, creating a flat to inverted yield curve. Although the interest rates were higher for the short term, they were actually lower for the longer term bonds.

The Utility Average can be misleading at times. Severe weather can cause sudden increases in earnings, dividend capture plays can run the stocks up, or buyout situations can occur. All of these can help to cause an unreliable reading of the Average as an indicator. However, in most cases, the Average can be useful as an indicator of interest rate movement and an indicator which confirms the direction of the other Dow Averages.

Market Volume

Volume, at times, can be a misunderstood indicator, even though nearly every investor has some understanding of its importance. There is, however, a simple differentiation that provides logic to fit the analysis of most volume situations.

Low Volume: Few players and not much interest in market plays.

High Volume: Many players and a great deal of interest in buying and/or selling stocks.

These facts are most of what really should be understood about volume, although volume statistics can give more information about the investor sentiment of the "broad" market.

Louis Rukeyser, the host of television's "Wall Street Week," has a good explanation of the importance of volume:

> Volume, as it happens, is closely watched by practically all the market's traders (as opposed to investors) because of the clues it affords to the market's essential sentiments.[3]

Volume is important to watch because it is watched by the "power players" or the "heavy hitters"; that is, by those who have the talents and the assets to make the big market moves. But, how does this actually relate to the individual investor? Rukeyser continues:

> If the market is rising and volume is heavy, it means that the great bulk of investors is optimistic—while an increase on light volume might be written off as purely technical and unconvincing. The

same would be true on the downside; if volume is heavier on the days the market is declining, this would be taken as a strongly negative signal.[4]

This is an explanation which is easy to understand and it sticks to the basic application of volume as an indicator. Essentially this is correct as it stands. However, as it can be said of any indicator considered in and of itself, it may not be true all the time. Here is a note of caution when considering the indications of volume:

> Tradition has it that increasing volume on rallies and decreasing volume on declines are signs of a healthy situation, but often that is not the case. Sluggish markets can be deadly, and the wildest volume fling of a rally may occur right at the top. Don't accept conventional wisdom unquestioningly; consider the significance behind the statistics.[5]

This again stresses the importance of considering more than one indicator in any investment strategy. Each indicator is merely a small part of the whole picture of the market. Tracking the indicators and noting changes in them can give the investor a feel for the market swings.

The graph in Exhibit 2 shows the direct relationship which can exist between volume and market rallies or declines. If one compares this graph with the Dow Industrials (page 83) for the same time period, the rise in volume and the rise in the market coincide. Declines in volume when the market is dropping can also be readily observed.

Volume has one other significance that has not yet been discussed: investor sentiment. During any given trading day, the broker, or individual investor who has a quote machine, can view the total volume as well as up volume, down volume, and unchanged volume. This is an excellent broad market view of investor sentiment. At a glance, it indicates the strength of the market and whether the broad market is doing more selling or buying.

Volume is an important indicator, but it is important for the investor to understand the motivating factors behind the current volume trends. This information can be found in the news media. An understanding of volume can help an investor understand why the market is moving in its current trend.

Exhibit 2 New York Stock Exchange Volume

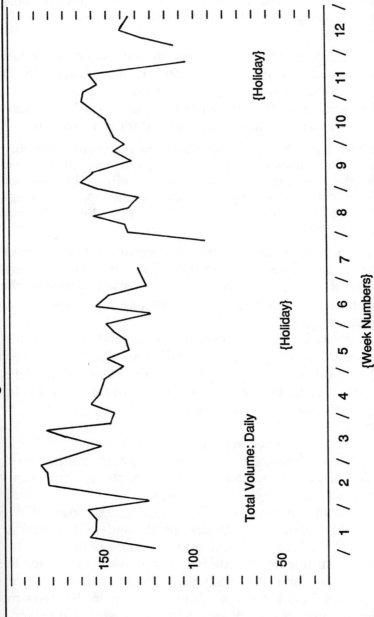

Total volume of shares traded on the New York Stock Exchange October through December 1988. (Volume in Millions)

New Highs And New Lows

Each day of trading produces a number of stocks which reach a new high for the year and a number of stocks which fall to a new low. These numbers are totaled and appear in the financial news.

New highs and lows can be an indicator of continued upward strength in the stock market or they can indicate a growing weakness. If, on a particular trading day the figures look something like this:

New Highs: 34
New Lows: 7

The uptrend for the day was bullish and is likely to continue. If the difference between the two numbers begins to narrow, another kind of signal may become evident.

	Mon.	*Tue.*	*Wed.*	*Thur.*	*Fri.*
New Highs	34	28	20	26	20
New Lows	7	15	19	23	20

The steady weakening in the number of new highs can be a signal of a weakening in the primary trend. This may mean that the market is about to turn in direction.

A sudden surge in new highs can signal an approaching rally. Many times it is a change in the new high and new low relationship which gives an early warning signal to an approaching turn or correction and, conversely, a possible renewed stock rally.

Because there are few absolutes in the stock market and because many investors are scrutinizing any and all indicators, the signals given may be overridden by other factors. When the signals are canceled out by other actions it is best to consider the signal as incorrect and move on to the other indicators and the action in progress.

The new highs and new lows indicator is probably best considered as a signal which is a yellow caution light, rather than a red stop or green go light. When considered in this context the signals will be more helpful in planning changes in strategy.

Moving Averages

Moving average is an indicator which shows a smooth trend line for a specific time period: 10-day, 30-day or 200-day. As was discussed in Chapter One, the moving average can be helpful in determining the current direction of the primary trend. It enables the investor to see the effects of several days' trading at a glance.

The main weakness of the moving average is the distortion which can occur after a sudden and sharp move in the stock market. This is particularly true of the longer time period moving averages. They may continue to show a down trend when in actuality the trend has turned up in direction. This weakness can be taken into account by considering the actual movement of the averages and by looking at a shorter time period moving average.

According to William A. Remaley, professor of finance at Susquehanna University, "moving average trading systems are trend-following systems. That is, they signal a move in the market after the trend has changed. Thus, such systems are not expected to get an investor into the market at the exact bottom or out at the exact top. Rather, the systems are designed to keep an investor on the right side of the market for the longer trends. The longer the moving average, the slower the indicator is to signal a change in trend."[6]

This lagging tendency of the longer moving average also has an important advantage as compared to the shorter averages. It will give fewer "false signals," as the market moves. Again, professor Remaley.

"But a longer moving average also provides fewer false signals— a signal caused by abrupt but short-term, non-directional price variations. The shorter the moving average, the sooner it will signal a turn in the market; but more false alarms will be given in a market without strong trends. Thus, the use of a short-term average may lead to whipsawing—repeated small losses caused by frequent recurring signals to move into and out of the market."[7]

There are also times when the market averages are trading nowhere near their long-term moving averages. The market averages may be high above or far below the moving average. At these times, the longer moving average is of little use, therefore, if one is to use a moving average it must be a shorter term. The solution to the weaknesses seems to be consulting a combination of moving averages. Remaley concludes that "the DJIA 200-day moving average can be a useful tool, although not the only tool, for investors who are interested in timing the market."[8]

Standard & Poor's 500

The S&P 500 is a list of stocks assembled as a broad market index for the stock market. The index is "weighted" to reflect the market value of the companies. As stated by Howard J. Brown, in a recent S&P Stock Guide:

> Simply put, the price of each stock in the index is multiplied by the number of shares outstanding for that company, and that value for each of the 500 or 100 (S&P 100) issues is totaled. For the S&P 500 the total value of those stocks in the base period 1941-43 is given an index price of 10. The S&P 100 is calculated in a similar way with the index value of 100, set equal to the market value of the stocks on January 2, 1976. Therefore, after the issues are totaled, the resulting value is divided by the base divisor, to arrive at the index. For the more technically minded, the actual formula is:

$$\text{Index} = \frac{\Sigma P_1 Q_1}{\Sigma Po\, Qo} \times \begin{array}{l} 100 \text{ (for S\&P 100)} \\ \text{(or)} \\ 10 \text{ (for S\&P 500)} \end{array}$$

> Where P_1 represents the current market price, Po the market price in the base period, Q_1 the number of shares outstanding and Qo the number of shares outstanding in the base period, subject to adjustment when necessary to offset changes in capitalization Σ equals the sum of. The S&P 500 currently contains 462 NYSE, 29 OTC, and 9 AMEX stocks. The S&P 100 is exclusively NYSE."[9]

This gives some idea of what the S&P 500 is composed of, and how it is calculated. It provides another standard of measure, a benchmark to which one can compare the performance of a diversified portfolio of stocks. Many institutional investors use the S&P 500 as a benchmark for their annual performance.

The Standard and Poor's 500 index can be a broad market indicator due to its diversification. However, the "market weighted" quality can also cause the index to favor the large capitalization companies, the same companies which are listed in the Dow Averages.

A look at any comparison chart between the S&P 500 and the Dow Jones Industrial Average will point out that the index and the average have a definite tendency to track each other in major market moves. The large capitalization is the main reason, but stocks also tend to move in a group, especially when the move is a major one.

Although the DJIA and the S&P 500 tend to mirror each other in directional movement, the larger 500 index tends to somewhat moderate the volatility. An institutional investor managing a large portfolio of stocks needs a larger index with which to compare performance results. According to Albert S. Neuber, a manager for Standard & Poor's Corporation, "Investors would do well to compare the performance of the S&P 500 with that of the Dow before drawing conclusions about broad-based market moves."[10]

The S&P 500, like other market averages or indicators, is constantly changing. These changes, according to Neuber, can be important to the investor for many reasons: "Astute investors also keep track of the changing composition of the S&P 500. Changes in the index may reflect changing economic conditions and a growth in relative importance of various industries. In addition, changes in the composition of the index are indicative of changes in the composition of the stock market."[11]

This reinforces the idea of an ever-changing stock market, making comparisons of one year to another difficult and even questionable. In addition, "It is also interesting to note that stocks enjoy market gains and substantial increases in trading volume the day after their inclusion in the S&P 500, as many studies have shown."[12]

This might help to explain some of those mysterious increases in individual stock prices, which occur from time to time. As Neuber explained, "Professionally managed index funds are the cause of this boost in performance. These portfolios are designed for large institutional players to mirror the market and thereby equal its performance; currently, there is over $121 billion invested in these

Exhibit 3   Dow Industrials and S&P 500

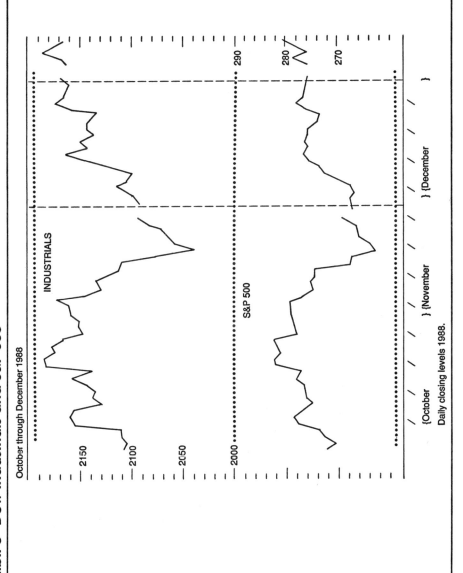

October through December 1988

INDUSTRIALS

S&P 500

{October   }{November   }{December   }

Daily closing levels 1988.

funds, of which approximately $70 billion is invested in index
funds based on the S&P 500. When a new firm is added to the S&P
500, these funds must purchase significant amounts of the added
stock to reflect the new composition of the index."[13]

This information points out how important the S&P 500 Index is
to the institutional investor as well as to the individual investor.
There is a very large amount of money in motion with the investors
who make use of the S&P 500. Therefore, it is an indicator worthy
of consideration when looking at moves and trends in the stock
market.

ENDNOTES

[1] *Timing the Market*, by Curtis M. Arnold and Dan Rahfeldt; Weiss
Research, Inc. p. 113; Probus Publishing Co., 1986.

[2] *When to Sell*, by Mamis and Mamis; Simon & Schuster/Fireside,
1986; original copyright 1977, pp. 118, 119.

[3] *How to Make Money in Wall Street*, by Louis Rukeyser; Doubleday;
Dolphin, 1976, pp. 111–112.

[4] Ibid.

[5] *When to Sell*, by Mamis and Mamis, Simon & Schuster/Fireside,
1986; original copyright 1977, p. 121.

[6] "Moving Averages as Market Timing Indicators" by William A.
Remaley, professor of finance at Susquehanna University.
From an article appearing in *AAII Journal*, October 1987, p. 11.

[7] Ibid. pp. 11, 12.

[8] Ibid. p.14.

[9] *Standard & Poor's Stock Guide*, September 1988, p. 2.

[10] "The S&P 500," by Albert S. Neuber, manager of research and
index services for Standard & Poor's Corporation. Taken from
an article appearing in the *AAII Journal*, January, 1987, p. 15.
The *AAII Journal* is published by the American Association of

Individual Investors, 625 N. Michigan Avenue, Suite 1900, Chicago, IL 60611.

[11] Ibid.

[12] Ibid.

[13] Ibid.

Chapter Nine

"Quick" Market Indicators

The Tick

The Tick, as an indicator, will tell an investor what is happening in the market right now. If a stock trades at a price higher than the previous trade, it is referred to as an "up tick." If it is trading at a price lower than the previous price the term used in description is "down tick." These terms are used to describe trades of individual stocks.

If all of the current down ticks (of the trades of individual stocks) are put together and subtracted from the up ticks, the resulting calculation is the "cumulative tick." In stock market lingo, this is referred to simply as the "tick." The tick is figured on all of the stocks trading on the New York Stock Exchange.

The significance of the current tick is a matter of degree. Between the levels of −100 tick to +100 tick, it is considered to be rather insignificant and in neutral territory. Levels exceeding these neutral limits can be instantly indicative of the market's current direction and give some idea as to the momentum of the trend. Since this is a broad market indicator of all the New York Stock Exchange stocks, it may disagree with the market Averages at any given time. At times, this may be an early warning of a turn in the market. At other times, the tick may quickly reverse and line up with the Averages.

One occasion where the tick seems to disagree with the market averages is when the market stages a sudden rally. The Dow Industrials may be up 15 or 20 points, but the tick may be showing –150 or –200. The most probable reason for the phenomena is this. As the market surges upward, limit sell orders are activated, causing enough selling to create the negative tick. If the market continues to advance upward, the tick eventually comes in line on the positive side.

The tick can also suggest the existence of "programmed trading," where computers are activating buys or sells of large blocks of stock. A level of 300 or more generally signifies the existence of this type of trading. A +400 tick can indicate programmed buying, whereas –350 could be the beginning of some programmed selling. Institutional traders are also watching the tick; they do not want to miss out on an important rally or be left holding the bag in a sharp decline.

In a panic sell situation, the tick becomes rather meaningless. It only confirms what is already known: everyone is selling.

Although the meanings of the numbers of the Tick are not absolute, they are worth checking when placing a trade, as they can give an indication of the strength and momentum of the immediate market move.

The Trin

The Trin, also called the "Short-Term Trading Index," is a measure of buying and selling pressure. It compares the advancing and declining stocks to the advancing and declining volumes. The formula for the trin looks like this:

The number of issues advancing in price
[divided by]
The number of issues declining in price
[equals a number, which is then divided by]

Total up volume [divided by] Total down volume

As an example; this might be the Trin at mid-morning on the New York Stock Exchange for a given trading day.

$$\frac{\begin{array}{c}\text{Total issues of stock advancing} = 600 \\ \text{[divided by]} \\ \text{Total issues of stock declining} = 300 \\ \text{Equals: 2}\end{array}}{\begin{array}{c}\text{Total up volume} \quad 30{,}000 \\ \text{[divided by]} \\ \text{Total down volume } 10{,}000 \\ \text{Equals: 3}\end{array}}$$

2 divided by 3 = .67

Because this number (.67) is less than 1.0, it indicates the existence of buying pressure.

Trin of less than 1.0 indicates buying pressure, while trin of more than 1.0 indicates selling pressure. Once again, the numbers are not absolute. A trin level of .90 to 1.10 is rather neutral. This is another broad market indicator, taking into account all of the stocks traded on the New York Stock Exchange.

The trin tends to move by degrees. It may open at 1.50, then start dropping as buyers come on the scene. It may drop to 1.35, then a few minutes later to 1.30, and within an hour or so be neutral at 1.0. There is usually a tendency for a trend like this to continue. There will also be times when the selling pressure returns and the trin will increase to 1.0 or higher.

The tick and trin figures from the trading day December 14, 1988, show the market in a selling mood. Even though the Dow Industrials were edging upward from about 10:00 in the morning, the Transportation was only lightly participating, and the broad market was tending toward the other direction. The cumulative tick was negative until the final hour of trading, and the trin was maintaining a neutral to slightly negative status. The negative tick suggests the beginning of selling programs at 1:00 P.M., which continued until 3:00 P.M. The turn of the cumulative tick is rather sudden, but may have had as much as an hour to change course from selling to buying. The Trin is relatively neutral for most of the day, only indicating a build in selling pressure between 2:00 P.M. and 3:00 P.M. This neutrality, in the face of a declining Dow Industrial Average and growing negative Tick, was also a factor in the last hour rally.

Exhibit 1   Dow Industrials; Tick and Trin

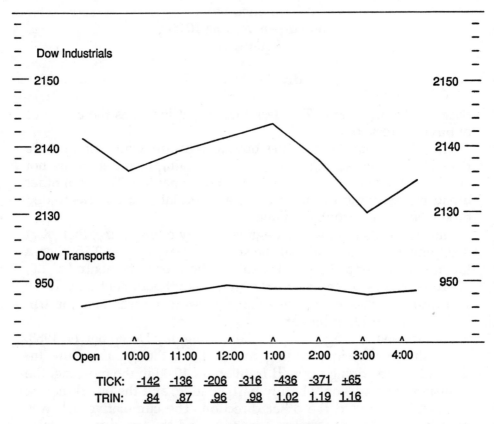

	Open	10:00	11:00	12:00	1:00	2:00	3:00	4:00
TICK:		-142	-136	-206	-316	-436	-371	+65
TRIN:		.84	.87	.96	.98	1.02	1.19	1.16

Hourly Trading figures from December 14, 1988.

TICK: Minus means more stocks being sold.
Plus means more stocks being bought.

TRIN: 1.0 and higher means selling pressure.
Less than 1.0 means buying pressure.

A stronger trin, up around 2.0 or higher, could have helped to cause a stronger selloff, and there would probably not have been a last hour rally.

This could have been a good day to buy stock. A viable strategy might have been to place a buy limit order in the morning, and check in the final hour to possibly change to a market order.

The decline in the broad market is further enhanced by checking the volume figures. The total volume for December 14, was 132,000,000 shares traded. The up volume was 44.7 million, and the down volume rose to 61.7 million. The number of shares unchanged was 25.9 million. The volume was a light trading day, but had some recognizable action from sizable stock traders.

Notice the strength in the Transportation Average. Even though the Dow Industrials began a selloff at about 1:00 P.M., the Transports hardly participated. This strength was a factor in the Industrials rally in the last hour of trading.

Understanding and observing the trin when placing a buy or sell transaction can provide some insight as to where the market is likely to be heading for the next few minutes or hours. This can help the investor decide whether to place an order and if the order should be a limit order or a market order.

Advance—Decline—Unchanged

Many investors follow the advance/decline, or A/D line, as it is often called, but many people forget about the unchanged stocks. Unchanged stocks are those stocks which are trading at the same price as the previous day's close; they are those stocks where the number of buyers is currently equal to the number of sellers.

The unchanged category also has its own index which can be calculated by dividing the number of issues unchanged during a particular day, by the total number of stocks traded. The percentage resulting will usually vary in a range between 5 percent and 25 percent. The readings are considered bullish at the low end of the scale and more bearish near the high end. Obviously, if the number of stocks closing at the same price as the previous day is increasing, it can be a "toppish" signal. The unchanged issues can also help to keep the advance/decline picture in better perspective.[1]

Exhibit 2 Advanced—Decline—Unchanged

12/16/88

	Industrials:	+17.71	Total Volume:	196.5 Million	
—	Transports:	+ 6.19	Up Volume:	126.8 Million	—
—	Utilities:	+ 1.13	Down Volume:	37.3 Million	—
			Unchanged Volume:	32.3 Million	—

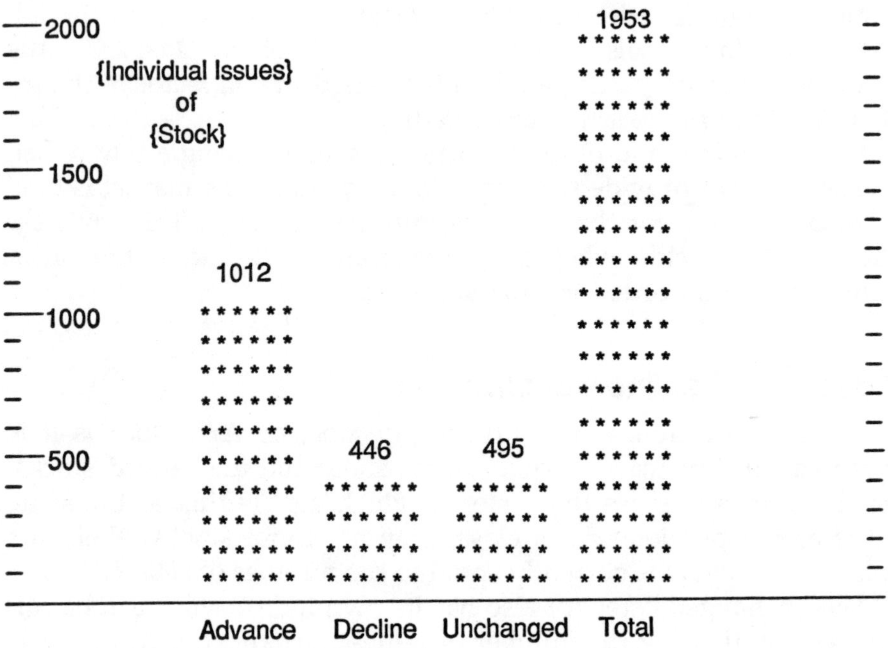

```
—2000                                    1953
 —                                      * * * * * *
 —        {Individual Issues}           * * * * * *
 —              of                      * * * * * *
 —            {Stock}                   * * * * * *
—1500                                   * * * * * *
 —                                      * * * * * *
 —                                      * * * * * *
 —                                      * * * * * *
 —            1012                       * * * * * *
 —                                      * * * * * *
—1000     * * * * * *                    * * * * * *
 —        * * * * * *                    * * * * * *
 —        * * * * * *                    * * * * * *
 —        * * * * * *                    * * * * * *
 —        * * * * * *                    * * * * * *
—500      * * * * * *    446      495    * * * * * *
 —        * * * * * *  * * * * * * * * * * * * * * * * *
 —        * * * * * *  * * * * * * * * * * * * * * * * *
 —        * * * * * *  * * * * * * * * * * * * * * * * *
 —        * * * * * *  * * * * * * * * * * * * * * * * *

          Advance    Decline  Unchanged   Total
```

Graph showing the relationship between the stocks which advanced, declined or were unchanged during the trading day on December 16, 1988.

Exhibit 2 shows a day when the Dow Industrials rallied 17.71 points. (December 14th, when the market had a nine point decline, would have been a good day to buy.) The Transports were in line with a gain of 6.19 and the Utility Average also up 1.13. Notice on the graph the strength of advancers over decliners by a ratio of more than 2 to 1. This is a healthy ratio, but the truly strong ratios are in the 3 to 1 or even 5 to 1 areas.

Advances and declines are also broad market indicators. When they are observed during the trading day, they can give some indication of where the broad market is heading in terms of the numbers of different stock issues traded. (Volume is just an indication of volume being traded; it does not distinguish individual issues or companies.)

If the advances outnumber the declines by a 3 to 1 or 4 to 1 ratio, the action is strongly bullish for the entire market. If this ratio begins to narrow and becomes less than 2 to 1, it can be the signal of a top or possible correction. The market could turn suddenly and head down. The opposite can hold true in a declining market.

Advance/Decline Line

A simple mathematical formula creates the indicator known as the advance/decline line. It is figured by merely subtracting one from the other, this daily figure is then subtracted from a running figure to complete the calculation. Perhaps "the bathtub analogy" explains it best.

> Picture the market as a bathtub and the water level is represented by the advance/decline line. Advancing stocks raise the water level and declining stocks lower the water level. Market strength or weakness is determined by that water level.[2]

As an indicator, the advance/decline line tends to work best at picking the top of an advance, as opposed to signaling the bottom. This is probably due to the decline of buying frenzy as a top is reached. As the buying frenzy subsides, traders are getting ready to sell and take their profits. At the bottom, even though a panic or decline may be over, buyers are cautious about resuming their buying activities. They want to be certain that the bottom has been reached. They will often wait a while and slowly begin to rebuild positions.

A look at the advance decline line in Exhibit 3 suggests that the market bottomed out in week eight, and then began its climb back up. Actually the market started up a week or so earlier. It can take the A/D line a while to catch up to the turns. A look at the line can help the investor sort out all of the short-term rallies and declines which may be occurring in the market and get some idea of current market direction. Like other indicators it should be considered as only part of the picture.

Whether an investor watches the progress of the advance/decline line for technical analysis, or uses advances-declines-unchanged to see where the day might be headed, it is important to remember that the strength of a rally of a bull market is easily observed by watching the degree to which advancers outnumber decliners to see if that distance is widening (showing increasing strength) or becoming more narrow (showing signs of weakness).

ENDNOTES

[1] *Timing the Market,* by Arnold and Rahfeldt, pp. 88–89.

[2] Ibid, pp. 86–87.

Exhibit 3   Advance—Decline Line

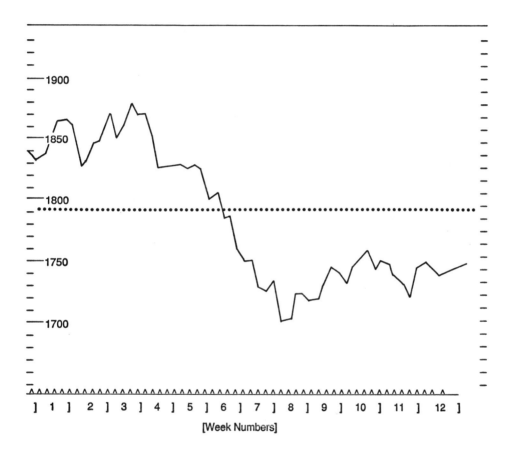

Advance/Decline Line tracking October through December 1988. Figures based on stocks advancing in price minus stocks declining in price, on the New York Stock Exchange.

Chapter Ten

Some Economic Indicators

Toward the end of January of 1989, just after the presidential inauguration of George Bush, a person could walk by a newsstand and see three seemingly contradictory headlines.

"Inflation Will be Controlled"
"Interest Rates Expected to Rise"
"Stock Market Rallies to Post-Crash High"

The control of inflation and a rise in the stock market can go together, but generally, as interest rates rise, the stock market falls.

This seems to be a time when investors and others must be flexible and somewhat philosophical in considering the state of the economy. Whenever economic claims are stated, one needs to relate the claims, or statements, to the action taking place in the stock market.

In 1985, the goal was to curb inflation by weakening the dollar. This would also be favorable to the stocks of companies that depended on large exports of their finished goods. So the dollar fell. Stocks rose significantly, and inflation, though not eliminated, was brought under some control. Now, in 1989, the experts are saying that in order to control inflation, we need more strength in the dollar.

Obviously, the dollar fell too low. Many factors which have an effect on the economy can be only partially controlled and fine-tuned for top performance.

The economy of the country might be thought of as a finely tuned carburetor which needs constant adjustment. If the mixture of gasoline and air is too rich the engine stalls and won't run. If the mixture is too lean, there won't be enough combustible material for the engine to run. In the economy, if there is too much money available at low cost, too much product is produced. If interest rates are high and there is not enough capital available, a shortage of goods can develop. Either situation can lead to a recession and a stalled economy. Although this sounds simple enough, it isn't quite that easy. Once an adjustment is made, any number of variables can alter the actual outcome. An action which began as a solution to a particular problem, will often end up being part of the problem. This gives some idea as to why the economy is so very difficult to control.

Like the stock market, the economy has continued to grow and expand. Understanding the various aspects of the economy is a difficult proposition, even for the experts. In 1989, the situation has become even more difficult to understand due to the effects of global implications on the economy.

In order to understand these alterations it is necessary to be well aware of the current economic themes. Only by studying and analyzing the daily news and information can an individual investor hope to keep up with the changes. It is important to know and understand the economic change, and to notice the impact of that change. There have been several occasions when economics experts have indicated an approaching recession which failed to materialize.

In the mid-seventies, a statement was heard that the economists had predicted five of the last *three* recessions.

After the stock market crash of 1987 many experts said we were heading swiftly toward a sharp recession. The time frame given was six months to one year. But it didn't happen. The recession didn't appear and the stock market recovered. In the early part of 1989 the economic debate was how far away the elusive recession might be. This tells us how difficult it can be to understand economic developments. Even though economic developments can be difficult to interpret, they should be noticed and observed for their impact.

Statements made regarding the economy are important: Economists can be right at times. Also, the statements themselves can be as important as the developments which materialize. There are times when the market reacts more to what is being said about the economy than it reacts to what the economy is actually doing.

For example, through the last half of 1988, much of the positive news regarding business (increase in profits, expanding markets, and lower unemployment) actually had a negative impact on the stock market. The reason given for this impact was that all of the normally good news was a sign of a heating up of the economy. This suggested that inflation was just around the corner, with a strong recession right behind.

Good news had actually become bad news. Understanding the economic news was like trying to fly an airplane upside down. Good was bad and bad could be good. At least a couple of market rallies were accompanied by an increase in interest rates and a military skirmish. These kinds of events will often cause a drop in the stock market.

The market reacts to various economic situations and stimulations. It does not necessarily react in a predictable way with each new change.

The individual investor can delve into economic theory and analysis as time and interest permits. Those investors who have less time and interest can maintain a basic understanding of the current economic developments and make use of some technical analysis in conjunction with the Dow Theory. This will assist the investor and give him at least a few advantages when approaching the stock market.

Here is a brief list of some of the economic indicators which often have an effect on the stock market.

- Interest rates
- Strength of the dollar
- Federal budget deficit
- Trade deficit
- Leading economic indicators
- Defense spending

A detailed list could go on at some length. The important thing is noticing how the news of the change in status of economic indicators affects the stock market and the signals given by the stock market indicators.

The reality of economic changes is how these changes affect the life of the individual. If an inflationary trend is found primarily in real estate, and the individual is currently a homeowner, that person is not as directly influenced by the inflation. On the other hand if an inflationary trend is accelerated in food products or clothing, everyone is obviously going to have some changes in lifestyle.

If economic changes impact employment, they quickly become an economic reality for the people involved, but not necessarily for others. A rise in unemployment is not as meaningful to those still employed, although increasing unemployment can be a forecast of a slowdown in the overall economy. This possible slowdown can be positive if the economy has been recently overheating.

To the individual investor, the economic reality is the effect of economic changes on the style of investing undertaken. The short-term trader gambles on the changes in the economy. The long-term trader certainly notices the effects, but, generally, only for a limited period of time. Whether an investor is long or short term in trading, some understanding of economic changes and their impact on the stock market can improve the profits and growth of investments.

Interest Rates

Most people are aware that interest rates change. However, many are not aware of how interest rates change. Changes in interest rates are determined by the price of government bonds, which are regularly issued and traded every day. The price of the bonds being traded determines the current interest rate. If bond prices are falling, interest rates are rising. This generally means that stock prices are also falling. The opposite is also true as bond prices rise, interest rates fall.

Two other factors influencing interest rates and the prices of bonds are the Fed Funds Rate and the Federal Discount Rate. The Fed Funds Rate is the interest rate charged between banks when they borrow money from each other that is drawn from funds on deposit at the Fed. The Federal discount rate is what banks pay to borrow funds from the Fed. The Federal Reserve Bank sets the discount rate and can influence the Fed funds rate, but does not control it directly.

Another factor, the prime rate, is directly influenced by changes in Fed funds. The prime rate is more familiar to investors and others, due to the amount of publicity it receives. It is the interest rate charged by lending institutions to their major borrowers.

As changes are made in the Federal Discount Rate they are accompanied by some kind of announcement. The announcement is, at times, more important than the actual change because it gives the reason for the change. The reason given can be a valuable assessment of the current economic direction.

It should also be noted that it is possible for the Fed funds rates to rise and fall while the Federal discount rates remain unchanged. This can also cause a situation where the discount rate is raised and has no impact on the stock market. In this situation, the increase was simply adjusting to the Fed Funds Rate and the stock market had already discounted the increase.

A change in interest rates is one of the most important economic indicators of what is likely to happen in the stock market. Although the stock market may not always react consistently, changes in interest rates have a direct effect on market direction.

Strength of the Dollar

Strength of the U.S. dollar is often measured principally against the Japanese yen, although other monetary systems can also play a key role (i.e., pound sterling, Deutschmark, French franc, and others). Monetary fluctuations occur on a continual basis and can have varying economic impacts. The current strength of the dollar makes headlines for major moves and trends. When the monetary exchange rates are relatively balanced they become a rather neutral economic event and therefore not newsworthy.

Often, a major market move is credited to a strengthening or weakening of the dollar. The individual investor should consider news of the dollar's strength an important indicator of the strength of the stock market. Market reaction is often sudden and sharp. For example, the later part of 1988 had many market moves which were credited to the fluctuation of the dollar, particularly on the weak side.

On November 16, 1988, the Dow Industrials dropped more than 38.5 points. The fall was due to a number of factors, but the headlines of the day credited the fall to a drop in the dollar. On January 23 of 1989, the Dow Industrials were off 16.97 points, and the dollar's fall again received much of the blame. On the positive side, on January 27, 1989, the dollar moved up with some significance, and the Dow Industrial Average followed suit with a gain of nearly 32 points.

This volatility can make investment timing difficult for the individual investor. A newsline wire service would be of particular value in this situation. If the instant news is not available, the investor can depend more on noticing the periods of volatility and stability in the dollar's fluctuation. When the dollar is highly volatile, the investor can adjust investment strategies to take advantage of the situation, or he can totally avoid trading during these unpredictable periods of time.

Federal Budget Deficit

Debt increases by the federal government have a definite impact on the economy. When the government is borrowing more money it decreases the funds available for corporations to borrow. This tends to cause an upward pressure on interest rates and can increase inflation. The deficit is also magnified by the interest which must be paid on the money borrowed.

Decreasing the deficit can have some positive impact on the economy, however it can also mean less government spending and higher taxes which, in turn, can have a negative effect for the short term. Some believe that the two scenarios have a partially neutralizing effect on the deficit situation. Others believe that a zero deficit is the only way to maintain a stable economy. It is probably more important to understand how this deficit argument is impacting the stock market than it is to be on either particular side of the argument.

Trade Deficit

Are we importing more goods than we are exporting, and by how much? A decrease in the trade deficit tends to be good news for the market, and an increase tends to not be good. At times, this information becomes so sensitive that the market will react strongly to a "...less than expected increase." Trends in the deficit are important as they are a factor relating to the gross national product (GNP) and, therefore, are part of the productivity of the nation.

Leading Indicators

A monthly composite report of the current status of the 12 leading economic indicators is published by the U.S. government. This report appears in the financial press and other news media. The 12 leading economic indicators are:

- Average workweek, production workers, manufacturing hours
- Layoff rate, manufacturing
- New orders for consumer goods and materials
- Vendor performance, percentage of companies which are reporting slower deliveries
- Net business information
- Contracts and orders for plants and equipment
- New building permits, private housing units
- Net changes in inventories
- Change in sensitive prices
- Changes in total liquid assets
- Stock prices of 500 common stocks
- Money supply

This information comes out toward the end of the month for the previous month. Although it is considered reasonably reliable, the report has the reputation of predicting recessions which did not occur. This is probably due to an unforeseen change which was not accounted for in the statistics.

An investor can follow some or all of the 12 leading indicators on an individual basis, or follow the trend of the index of leading economic indicators.

Defense Spending

Nearly everyone seems to want a decrease in defense spending. The fact is, this decrease could have an economic impact on the country: a very large number of people are employed due to defense spending, and a decrease of significant proportions could cause a noticeable amount of unemployment.

At times, defense spending increases (or decreases) are a big issue getting a lot of play in the press and causing a certain amount of tremors on Wall Street. At other times, it appears to be a non-issue with little or no impact. It seems to be the possibility of change which determines the current importance of this issue.

Some economic indicators are more reliable than others, due to political influences or other more evolutionary factors. Economic reports can be constructed politically, or timed so they are released with more acceptable impact. One of the primary evolutionary factors of the economy is a trend toward globalization. It is a trend most certain to increase in the future. The transition to a global economy is generally acknowledged to be a positive move, but it could increase the difficulty of economic forecasting.

The stock market is affected by changes in the economy, and also by the announcements of changes in the economic indicators. The investor who is aware of these changes is better equipped to make sound investment decisions.

Chapter Eleven

Market Strength

What is the current strength of the stock market? Is it rising to new relative highs on heavy up-volume versus down-volume, with advances outnumbering declines by a two to one margin or better? Is the market having trouble reaching new highs, with the declining stocks gradually overtaking the advancing stocks? Are the numbers of new highs increasing and the numbers of new lows declining, or is the gap between them narrowing? Are other market indicators lining up in such a way as to confirm market strength, or is the confirmation weak and showing signs of divergence? Are interest rates staying level or declining, and are the other economic indicators remaining strong?

Strong Market

A classic strong up market is not particularly difficult to recognize, even for the casual observer. The new highs are there, the market may occasionally correct, but it soon recovers. The Transportation Average is consistently confirming the Dow Industrial's every move and, at times, surpassing it. Even the Utility Average tows the line and acts as another confirming indicator. It is difficult to find an indicator which is not giving a positive reading. The economic news is positive and the interest rates are dropping slightly. There just do not seem to be any problems developing in the stock market.

At times like these, it becomes difficult for the investor to even keep an eye on all of the indicators. They keep showing the same positive picture. Bad news, if it appears, is washed away in the next rally. The only direction is up and when the next major move occurs, it will likely be a very strong up surge.

Some investors might say this is the top of the current trend. Others might believe that this is only the beginning. The Dow Theory followers would say that the market is strong, but it is time to closely watch the indicators for signs of weakness. As the signs of weakness develop, it is time to look for an indication of turning in the market. All of this sounds easy enough, but it is often not so easy.

The problem arises in determining if the signs of weakness are giving reliable signals. There will be times when the signals are completely ignored by the market activity, and other times when they are totally accurate.

The strong market is easily recognized, but it is also a time to begin looking for signals of developing weakness. Recognizing and understanding the meaning of these important signals is important for the individual investor. Every substantial rally must be examined for signs of developing weakness, signals which will precede a correction. Although it is possible to have a market rally which does not show an immediate correction, a top will eventually be reached, and the market will adjust in a downward direction.

Weak Market

New Highs versus New Lows

A decline in the number of new highs achieved by individual stocks, as compared to the number of new lows, can be an early warning of a turn in the stock market. It stands to reason that, if the market is consistently reaching new highs, the number of stocks reaching new highs should also be consistently above the number of new lows.

In some advancing markets the first signal of weakness will come from this area. The number of new highs each day will start to decline. Eventually, the new lows will start to increase and the turn in the market follows.

New highs versus new lows can be a helpful early warning signal at times. Other times, it can fail to give a signal (the lack of a signal can be especially true in a highly volatile market), or it may even give a false signal (brought on by simple short-term profit taking). Although this signal, in itself, may not be completely reliable, it is still worth keeping an eye on for those signs which may be confirmed elsewhere.

Advance-Decline-Unchanged

These three figures, stated during and at the end of the trading day, can give a reliable signal of weakness developing in the stock market. More precisely, the action relationship between them can signal the weakening.

When the market is strong, advancing stocks will outnumber decliners two to one or even three to one or more. However, if the number of unchanged stocks continues to grow, and the ratio between the advancing stocks and declining stocks begins to consistently narrow, a signal of a weakening market becomes evident.

This trend of weakening in the advance-decline-unchanged can be verified in the broad market indicator of volume, which shows advancing volume, declining volume, and unchanged volume.

Volume

Volume, as previously discussed, is a broad market indicator which can be viewed in terms of upward or downward action. Like the advance-decline-unchanged indicator, volume has the same parameters of up volume, down volume, and unchanged volume. It will show the weakening of a trend in much the same way as advancing and declining issues.

As the up volume begins to decrease, and the down volume and/or unchanged volume begins to increase, a weakness in the broad market is signaled. This signal will often precede a down turn in market prices. It must be remembered that volume is a broad market indicator. The volume indicator is best used in con-

junction with the advance-decline-unchanged indicator when looking for signals of weakness.

As with the new highs and new lows a misleading factor is a
tendency for volume indicators to give false signals of weakness
during periods of profit taking and times of relatively low total
volume. Although low total volume is an indication of weakness by
itself, it has a tendency to temporarily render other indicators unreliable. Without substantial volume of shares traded, all of the indicators become more difficult to interpret.

Lower volume itself can be a signal of weakness in the stock
market, but in most cases, low volume is a sign of indecisiveness on
the part of professional stock traders. This can be particularly true
in a slow-moving, lethargic market, where low volume has become
the norm.

Tick and Trin

The tick and the trin are worthy of mention in the signaling of a
weakening market for the very short term. If a particular trading
day is showing signs of being weak and a possible non-event, the
status of the tick and trin can be of assistance in verifying or deny-
ing this trend. If the market seems weak (up a point or down a
point) and the tick is a −425, the investor can be assured that the
action is likely to pick up. On the other hand, if the trin is showing
a .45, the market could be in a current stalemate, with the main
action to come later in the day. Keeping in mind the very short-
term nature of tick and trin can tell the individual investor the immediate market strength or weakness.

For the longer term signs of weakness one must turn to the
market averages. The averages are where the more traditional Dow
Theory concepts come into play.

Dow Industrial Average

The first sign of weakness appears when the Dow Jones Industrial
Average fails to reach a new high. It does not matter whether it is
profit taking, the minor fluctuation of a daily trend, the beginning
of a secondary trend, or a turn in the primary trend. The only important factor is the most immediate one. The market failed to
reach a new high. That failure is a signal of weakness. Whether the

weakness is continued in the next few days or weeks remains to be seen, but when it happens, it is real. (See Exhibit 1.)

Dow Transportation Average

If the weakness in the Dow Industrials is confirmed by a corresponding weakness (failure to reach new highs) in the Transportation Average, it becomes an even stronger signal. It is important that the investor keep in mind that the confirmation does not necessarily have to occur on the same day, although it should occur within a few trading days.

Dow Jones Utility Average

If the Utility Average follows suit and confirms the Industrials and Transports in showing weakness, it becomes an even stronger signal. It may be time to look for a sharp secondary reaction, or an actual turn in the primary trend. Also, it is important to keep in mind that the Utility Average (because of its sensitivity to interest rates) can be an early warning by itself.

Even though the Utility Average appeared to give a signal early in 1987, it was several months later before the actual turn occurred. Obviously, many investors did not believe the signal to be accurate.

There are two important times to look for weakness.

- When the market is strongly advancing and there are profits to be protected.

- When the market has been a balanced market and the investor is looking for buying opportunities.

Approaching market weakness in this light turns a disadvantage into an advantage.

Bellwether

Stock market "bellwether" stocks have been around probably for as long as investors have traded stocks. Investors always look to find that one particular company whose stock tends to turn before the rest of the market, that one stock which leads the market in a particular industry sector. Whether it is the leading bank stock, computer stock, or oil stock, bellwether stocks have certain special qualities which make all other similar stocks follow.

Various stocks have held the position of bellwether throughout the history of the stock market, with varying degrees of success. Some were banks such as the Bank of the United States or the Bank of New York. Others were railroads like the Erie or Union Pacific. Later it would be companies like Standard Oil of New Jersey or possibly General Electric.

In today's market, nearly everyone who follows the market has a custom set of bellwether stocks. The two most widely recognized are IBM and General Motors. To this might be added Exxon, and to some extent, AT&T. Stocks selected for this designation tend to be the leaders in their particular sector of industry. They are the larger capitalization companies, which may have some diversification, but not too much. A conglomerate which has become highly diversified becomes difficult to tie to any one particular industry sector; therefore, it is difficult to consider the company representative of other stocks.

There will be times during a bull rally when the market indicators remain strong. It can be very difficult to find signals of weakness and yet the investor has "a feeling" that the rally must turn at some point. During these times, the first signal of weakness may appear in the bellwethers. Their signals may be in a failure to participate, either by not showing as strong a rally or actually retreating in price. If the stock market continues its strength in the rally, the bellwethers will eventually join also. However, the failure of a bellwether to participate can cause the market to do some correcting before resuming the rally.

The cause of this phenomena is the institutional trader. The institution loves participating in a rally, but tends not to trust the constantly rising prices. This trader is looking for any possible excuse not to believe the major market move. As the lack of participation of the bellwether stocks is noticed, doubt begins to appear. Some traders may start to take profits, just in case the bellwether is correct. The market begins to lose ground. Other traders may recognize the cause to be bellwether queasiness. If the market still had strength once the effects of the bellwether were removed, bolder traders will begin to buy at what are now slightly depressed prices.

This can create a buying frenzy which can create even more strength in the market rally.

The individual investor should also notice the action of the bellwether stocks. Notice how, when, and if the market reacts to the bellwether and have one more possible insight in placing trades. If a weakness signal appears in one of the bellwether stocks, it is time to look for weakness in other indicators. If the other indicators remain strong, it is likely a false signal from the bellwether.

Basing investment decisions on the movement of bellwether stocks alone is probably unwise. There will be times when the bellwether is giving false signals and other times when a kind of manipulation may be occurring. However, using the bellwether as an observation point which may signal an early weakness in a rally can be a useful strategy. There are also signals given by the bellwether as to an approaching rally, although these signals may not be as reliable as the weakness signal.

The stock market will often give signals of strength and weakness. Signals, as such, can suggest a change in direction for the market, but they do not determine the course of the market. The course of the stock market is always determined by the activities of the buyers and sellers of stock.

Balanced Market

A balanced market is a slower moving market. It tends to gain slightly over time, with occasional corrections. It could also be called a slow moving bull market, in the sense that prices of stocks are rising. If they are not rising, they are at least remaining stable. If they do not remain stable or rise slightly, the market will rather quickly drop to a lower support level where stability can be achieved.

A certain sign of the balanced market is the increase in "dividend capture" stock plays. Stocks which pay dividends have an event which occurs every quarter of the year. This is a particular day which determines who will receive the dividend for that payment period. This is called the "Ex-Dividend Date."

Investors who wish to receive the dividend must purchase the stock prior to this ex-date. Sellers who wish to receive the dividend must not sell the stock until on or after the ex-date. This situation creates stock which is growing in value as the ex-date is approaching. On the ex-date, the price of the stock is reduced by the amount of the stock dividend which will be paid.

Large investors who can afford to buy blocks of several thousand shares may do so, only with the idea of capturing that dividend. They may also purchase other large blocks as the stock goes ex-dividend, due to the temporarily reduced price. Thus, on the one hand, they have received the income from the dividend in a short period of time, and, on the other hand, have purchased the stock at lowered prices.

This dividend-capture technique is a sure sign of a slow, lethargic, or balanced, stock market. If the technique is continued through a few dividend ex-dates, it can become a trading strategy for the individual investor. That is, to hold a stock and sell if a run up in price occurs shortly prior to the ex-date, or to place a low buy order on the ex-date and pick the stock up at a reduced price.

The ex-dividend play may work on some occasions. If it does not work, the cause may be too many other investors who have the same idea and strategy. As a market changes in strength, the dividend capture play becomes less evident. There are more interesting market moves for the institutions and other investors.

A balanced market is a period of accumulation and distribution of stock. A check of the advance/decline line and the up volume versus down volume, can tell the investor if the bias is on accumulation or distribution.

Dow Theory developer and former *Wall Street Journal* editor, William Hamilton, referred to this as "forming a line." There is no set formula as to how long a balance can exist in the stock market. It will last until some event or change in information causes more buyers or more sellers to come on to the scene.

A good portion of 1988 was a balanced market. Not many advances of significance, a few declines and a lot of dividend capture going on. The most bullish indication was observed in some of the few market "breaks" from the line. In the vast majority of cases, when the stock market broke, it broke to the upside with a significant increase in volume. Hamilton said this was a bullish sign in a slow market and it is still true today.

A look at the chart in Exhibit 1 of price movements of the Dow Industrial Average and the Transportation Average for the week of January 23, 1989, through January 27, 1989, shows an interesting rally. Monday began with a small rally, which weakened in the first hour of trading with the Dow Industrials. Notice that the Transportation Average did not follow the turn immediately. The Dow again tried a small rally, but by this time the Transports were falling. The day closed with the Dow Industrials down nearly 17 points and the Transportation Average Down just under two points. This is an important comparison, as the Transportation Average did not fall as much as did the Industrial Average. This fact suggests that the market should seek a higher level. The rest of the signals were mixed for the day. Declining stocks outnumbered advancing stocks by nearly two to one, which is negative. The number of new highs was 57 and new lows was 12 (positive). The up volume was 22 million shares and the down volume was 88.5 million shares (negative). The total volume was a moderate 141.6 million shares (positive, heavier volume would make this negative), the closing tick was –462 (negative), and the trin closed at 1.62 (somewhat negative). The two most positive signals were:

- The strength in the Transportation Average.
- The light to moderate volume.

In this situation, these two factors were the overriding signals which said the market was likely at a support level. The proof of this would have to be observed in the early part of the following day.

There was obvious hesitancy in the first hour of trading of Tuesday, January 24th. The Transportation Average was showing the greatest strength. Then the Industrials staged a rally to new levels. The rally hesitated in the middle of the week, but the strength was maintained. The rally continued all the way to Friday.

In any stock market rally, there will be periods of profit taking; these periods can occur suddenly and can represent a turning point. A midday turning point generally suggests profit taking, rather than an actual turn.

Exhibit 1 Dow Industrials and Transports (1/23–27/89)

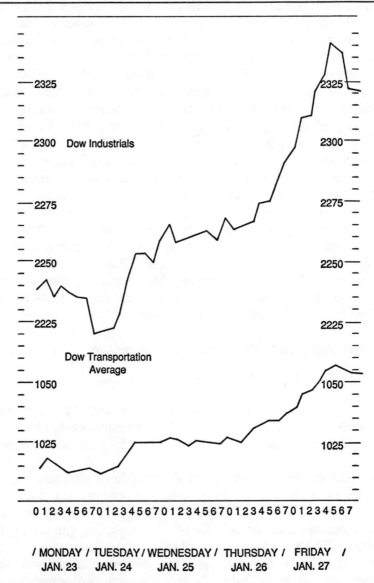

Hourly and daily tracking of the Dow Industrials and the Dow Transportation Averages 1/23/89 through 1/27/89.

The turning point on Friday, January 27th, can be easily observed on the chart. Both averages show a turn at about the same time. The confirmation is definite, even though the turn is stronger in the Industrials than in the Transports. It might be a turn which will continue to drop on Monday. An investor checking the hourly movement would be well aware of this information. However, an investor who only checked the closing Averages would believe the rally to be in force. In fact, the Dow closed at another relative new high (for seven months), up more than 31 points, with the Transportation Average up a strong 12.5 points. The midday turn on Friday the 27th indicated a couple of signals.

The first signal was the obvious one of a weakening rally, and the second was the first sign of profit taking in this rally. The Averages were still strong at the end of the day. A look at other indicators showed the following:

1. Utility Average: −.47 (negative)
2. S&P 500: +2.13 (positive)
3. New highs: 164 Previous: 512 (positive)
   New lows: 10 Previous: 31 (positive)
4. Advances: 929 Previous: 960 (positive)
   Declines: 611 Previous: 512 (negative)
   Unchanged: 467 Previous: 520 (positive)
5. Up volume: 175.9 million (positive)
   Down volume: 58.5 million (positive)
   Total volume: 254.9 million (positive)
6. Closing tick: −216 (negative)
7. Closing trin: .49 (positive)
8. Bellwethers: GM +1.75; IBM +.875 (lightly positive)

Only two of the indicators are giving a negative signal. The closing tick at −216 is only lightly negative. The narrowing of the advances to declines is a possible signal of weakness. The midday turn is also a possible sign of weakness in the rally. It is possible this same rally will resume on Monday. The importance of the confirmed turning point is likely to make investors nervous.

Exhibit 2 Dow Industrials and Transports (1/30–2/3/89)

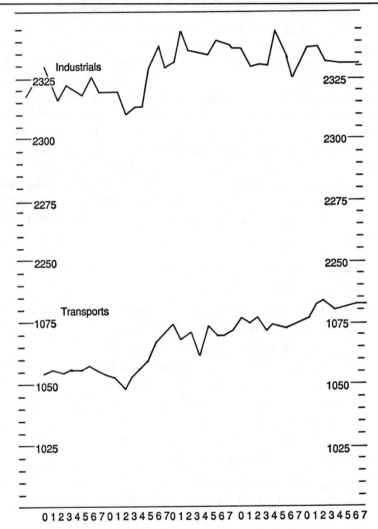

Industrials

2325

2300

2275

2250

Transports

1075

1050

1025

2325

2300

2275

2250

1075

1050

1025

0 1 2 3 4 5 6 7 0 1 2 3 4 5 6 7 0 1 2 3 4 5 6 7 0 1 2 3 4 5 6 7 0 1 2 3 4 5 6 7

/ MONDAY / TUESDAY / WEDNESDAY / THURSDAY / FRIDAY /
JAN. 30   JAN. 31   FEB. 1   FEB. 2   FEB. 3

Hourly and daily tracking of the Dow Industrials and the Dow Transportation
Averages 1/30/89 through 2/03/89.

A glance at the graph for the following week in Exhibit 2 shows the existence of some hesitancy. The market again appears balanced. Tuesday showed a decent rally, establishing a somewhat higher trading range all the way to Friday. Thursday showed a small amount of weakness with the Dow closing down 4.46 points. This was not confirmed by the Transportation Average, which closed up 6.16 points. The Utility Average closed up a somewhat neutral .42.

There were 92 new highs and five new lows on Thursday; this was down only slightly from Wednesday when there were 120 new highs and 14 new lows.

The total volume was moderate at 183 million shares traded. Up volume of 91.1 million shares, down volume of 65.3 million shares, and unchanged volume of 27 million shares traded, showed some weakness in the broad market. The tick closed on the positive side at + 188 and the trin weakly positive at .83. Advancing stocks confirm the weakness shown in the volume figures with Advances 771 and declines at 662, unchanged stocks closed at 535. IBM and General Motors were rather neutral in this situation.

Altogether, there suggests the possibility that Friday will be a down day. There are certainly signals of weakness developing.

A look at Friday, February 3, shows a situation similar to that of Thursday, signals of developing weakness are appearing, although they are mixed with other signals which suggest positive market strength. The Dow Industrials closed down 2.8 points, with the Transportation Average closing up 6.59 points. 93 new highs and five new lows is not really signaling any weakness. The Utility Average is showing only a slight weakness being down .42. The total volume showing a fairly small decline to 172.9 million shares. Up volume was 91.1 million shares, with down volume at 55.4 million shares and unchanged volume at 26.4 million shares. The volume picture obviously improved slightly on Friday, showing the existence of positive broad market sentiment. The closing tick was a neutral −59 and the trin was at .75. The weakness in the advances (792) as compared to the declines (642) and the unchanged issues at 518, was almost identical to the data on the previous day. IBM was off 5/8 (lightly negative) and GM neutral was unchanged.

Put this analysis together, and there is a suggestion that Monday could be a similar day, unless something unforeseen occurs. In fact, Monday, February 6, 1989, showed a drop in the Dow Industrials of 10.81 points, with more definite weakness developments.

- Up volume 63.3 million shares
- Down volume 66.6 million shares
- Advances 646 declines 778 unchanged 501
- IBM down 1 1/8, but GM up 1/4

These were definite signs of weakness. These signals do not necessarily tell the investor that the market will turn in direction, but they present a warning of indecisiveness in the movement of the market.

All of the cases described above involved mixed signals. The Dow dropped accordingly, though not by much. After the rally of the previous week, it would be in order for some market correction due to profit taking. Even this small profit taking provided some signals and clues as to what could happen next.

An investor, looking for weakness in the market indicators, will have some advantage in placing orders to buy and sell stock.

Chapter Twelve

A Contrarian View

In the early 1900s when Charles Dow wrote that "...a healthy skepticism is not out of place in the stock market...," he was partly stating the view of a contrarian.

The contrarian is always looking for something opposite to occur. When all the talk concerns inflation, the contrarian is not as concerned with its development. As inflation gathers speed, this investor can be seen preparing for a drop, perhaps strategically selling gold and buying stock. If the stock market is rising, this investor will often bet on the fall. When the stock market is falling, this investor sets strategy for a rally.

The contrarian will often sell short in a rising market, and buy long on a falling market. This is most evident when the market is near the high or low extremes of recent trading. It is the intention of the contrarian to be setting a strategy of opposition to the current sentiment.

The contrarian is the "devil's advocate" of the markets. Perhaps the greatest lesson to be learned by the individual investor is to always be asking questions like:

- What if the current sentiment is incorrect?

- How will a sudden change affect the market and individual stocks?

- What technical factors suggest that the current sentiment is likely to change soon?

- Why does gut instinct say a change is coming?

- What strategy can take best advantage of a turn in the market?

Contrarians tend to be technical analysts. Their main concern is the trend of the market, whether they invest in stocks, bonds, options, or commodities. The contrarian is looking for the trend to move to the extreme ranges of recent trading, a six-month new low or perhaps a seven-month new high. They are gambling on picking the turn in that trend. They are more speculative in their strategy, but can do well, even if they are correct only one out of five times.

Although the contrarian is mostly technical in his analysis of the stock market, investor sentiment is also a big concern. More specifically, the degree of investor bullishness or bearishness must be closely observed. Once again, this is looking for extremes. As the investor sentiment approaches relatively high levels of bullishness or bearishness, the contrarian is looking for the turn. With sentiment at 75 percent or 80 percent bullish, a strategy is set for a major correction in the market. As sentiment is becoming 60 percent to 70 percent bearish, the contrarian is looking for a rally.

It is important to note that the percentage numbers here are only listed as examples, they are not absolute. Each contrarian arrives at a unique percentage figure, based on his or her own analysis. These percentage figures may be changed for different market conditions. Whereas 80 percent bullish sentiment may be a reliable signal in one particular situation, a figure of 70 percent may be the signal in another time period. For these reasons, the contrarian makes use of analysis unique to the individual.

The individual investor can make use of some of the strategies of the contrarian. As the Dow Theory and the other stock market indicators become extremely bearish or bullish, a contrarian view might provide a counterbalancing strategy.

The market is known for reacting in unexpected ways. Good news comes out and the market drops; or, the market rises on bad news. In these situations, the market is said to have discounted the information ahead of the actual event. Likewise, when all of the indicators say that the market will fall, it might not. Or, when all of the indicators predict a strong rise, the opposite may occur. The

market has anticipated the news and reacted before the actual event
or news release. This discounting tendency of the market can become a problem if an investor is relying too heavily on market signals alone. A certain amount of a contrarian approach can also be
helpful in this situation by providing another perspective.

Market Sentiment: Bullish or Bearish

The investor can follow a certain amount of stock market sentiment
just by closely following some of the changes in the stock market
indicators. This is particularly noticeable in the volume, ad-
vance/decline and the more immediate tick and trin indicators.
Market sentiment can be observed in more detail by observing the
specific market sentiment indicators such as those listed in the
financial newspapers like *Investor's Daily.*

Referred to as the "Psychological Market Indicators," *Investor's
Daily*, lists 15 indicators of market sentiment.

1. Percent investment advisors bearish (50 percent = bullish; 20
   percent = bearish) percent investment advisors bullish (35
   percent bullish; 55 percent bearish)—investor's intelligence
2. *Wall Street Week Index* by R. Nurock (5 & more bullish; –5 &
   less bearish)
3. Odd lot short sales/odd lot sales
4. Public/NYSE specialist short sales (above 0.6 bullish; below
   0.35 bearish)
5. Short interest ratio (NYSE Short interest/avg. daily volume
   prior 30 days)
6. Ratio of price premiums on puts versus calls
7. Ratio of trading volume in puts versus calls
8. Mutual fund share purchases/redemptions (X-money market
   funds)
9. AMEX daily trading volume as percent of NYSE daily
   volume
10. OTC daily trading volume as percent of NYSE daily volume

11. Number of stock splits in *Investor's Daily* index (prior 30 days)
12. New issues in last 30 days as percent of all stocks on NYSE
13. Price-to-book value of Dow Jones Industrial Average
14. Price-to-earnings ratio of Dow Jones Industrial Average
15. Current dividend yield of Dow Jones Industrial Average

A glance at these "psychological market indicators" can give the investor a good idea of the current market sentiment with a different perspective. Figures are listed for the current status, as well as highs and lows for the past 5-year period and past 12-month period of time.

The week of February 6 through February 10, 1989, is a good example of how the "psychological indicators" can be helpful in maintaining perspective.

Monday, the 6th, began the week with some hesitation. The total volume was light, with more than 128 million shares being traded. Although the broad market held fairly strong (up volume 44.6 million, down volume 39.6 million), the Dow Industrials closed down just over 10 points. To some extent, the weakness which appeared on Monday was a continuation of the previous week. A positive signal was indicated by the Transportation Average which closed up 1.29 points. The drop in the Industrials was not confirmed.

Tuesday, February 7, came through with an ambitious rally. The Dow Industrials closed up 26.07 points on rather moderate volume of 148 million shares. The indicators were again giving fairly strong, bullish signals.

At this point, the market had rallied to a level which was considerably above the longer moving averages, many were beginning to look for another profit-taking correction. The correction came suddenly in a midday turn on Wednesday. The Transportation Average began to turn about an hour earlier than the Industrial Average, which peaked at about noon. The signals weakened and the market turned. The Industrials closed down only 3.93 points, but the Transportation Average closed down a more definite 11.81 points.

The turn was strongly confirmed this time, and the rest of the week continued to drop. An attempted rally early Thursday could not hold any strength of buyers. Obviously, the ideal profit-taking time was Wednesday. If an investor was not able to observe the midday turn as it occurred, the signals given at the close were still strong enough to say a correction was more than just a possibility.

The market continued to drop on Friday, closing down nearly 37 points with the Industrials and nearly nine points with the Transports. Volume was moderately heavy with 174 million shares traded. Most investors and analysts still believed this to be a profit-taking correction in a strong bull rally, but nearly all of the indicators were giving bearish signals. Some technical analysts were saying the time had come to sell and withdraw. The fundamentalists were a bit more positive. This was one time where an amount of contrarianism could be helpful.

If market indicators are going to be incorrect, the inaccuracy is most likely to occur in one of two situations.

- When *nearly all of the indicators* are giving the identical signal, (nearly all bullish or bearish)

- When the indicators themselves are highly volatile, flip-flopping back and forth, one day to the next. In this situation, the indicators are either indicating nothing, or a weakness developing which could become a downturn.

If an investor had looked at the "psychological indicators" on the following Monday, February 13, the picture would have been given a more accurate perspective. Although there were definite signals of weakness in the market, there was also a certain amount of stability.

Psychological Market Indicators 2/13/89

1. % Inv. Adv. Bears (50% = Bullish, 20% = Bear)

CURRENT /	5 YR. HIGH /	LOW:	1 YR. HIGH /	LOW
41.56%	55.3%	10.6%	55.3%	37.8%
	12/5/88	4/1/86	12/5/88	3/15/88

% Inv. adv. bulls (35% = bullish, 55% = bear)—
investor's intelligence

CURRENT /	5 YR. HIGH /	LOW:	1 YR. HIGH /	LOW
9.6%	68.3%	21.1%	48.0%	21.1%
	4/4/86	12/5/88	3/15/88	12/5/88

2. Wall Street Week Index by R. Nurock
    (5 & more bullish; –5 & less bearish)

CURRENT /	5 YR. HIGH /	LOW:	1 YR. HIGH /	LOW
–1	+8	–4	+6	–4
	11/6/87	7/28/88	2/15/88	7/28/88

3. Odd Lot Short Sales/Odd Lot Sales

CURRENT /	5 YR. HIGH /	LOW:	1 YR. HIGH /	LOW
.2.01%	36.1%	0.04%	26.9%	0.16%
	9/15/86	9/11/87	3/25/88	4/8/88

4. Public/NYSE Specialist Short Sales
    (Above 0.6 bullish: Below 0.35 bearish)

CURRENT /	5 YR. HIGH /	LOW:	1 YR. HIGH /	LOW
0.80	1.23	0.31	1.23	0.59
	5/13/88	10/23/87	5/13/88	4/1/88

5. Short Interest Ratio (NYSE Short Interest/Avg Daily
    Volume prior 30 days)

CURRENT /	5 YR. HIGH /	LOW:	1 YR. HIGH /	LOW
2.99	3.86	1.67	3.86	2.01
	12/30/88	2/17/87	12/30/88	3/10/88

6. Ratios on Price Premiums in Puts versus Calls

CURRENT /	5 YR. HIGH /	LOW:	1 YR. HIGH /	LOW
0.58	1.60	0.03	1.01	0.33
	2/17/87	10/19/87	1/31/89	5/23/88

7. Ratio on Trading Volume in Puts versus Calls

CURRENT /	5 YR. HIGH /	LOW:	1 YR. HIGH /	LOW
0.63	0.96	0.26	0.77	0.31
	12/3/87	10/21/87	5/11/88	4/12/88

8. Mutual Fund Share Purchases/Redemptions
   (X "except" Money Market Funds)

CURRENT /	5 YR. HIGH /	LOW:	1 YR. HIGH /	LOW
1.13	4.63	0.63	1.16	0.81
	10/1/85	10/30/87	2/8/88	8/1/88

9. AMEX Daily Trading Volume as % of NYSE Daily Vol.

CURRENT /	5 YR. HIGH /	LOW:	1 YR. HIGH /	LOW
6.44%	20.0%	2.56 %	15.1%	2.56%
	4/12/85	6/17 88	12/1/88	6/17/88

10. OTC Daily Trading Volume as % of NYSE Daily Vol.

CURRENT /	5 YR. HIGH /	LOW:	1 YR. HIGH /	LOW
76.4%	143%	35.6%	143%	38.8%
	5/20/88	12/9/87	5/20/88	1/25/88

11. Number of Stock Splits in *Investor's Daily* Index
    (prior 30 days)

CURRENT /	5 YR. HIGH /	LOW:	1 YR. HIGH /	LOW
54	211	34	77	34
	6/26/86	3/3/88	7/5/88	3/3/88

12. New Issues in Last Year as % of All Stocks on NYSE

CURRENT /	5 YR. HIGH /	LOW:	1 YR. HIGH /	LOW
153%	4.95%	1.32%	2.82%	1.32%
	3/5/87	10/19/88	2/9/88	10/19/88

13. Price-to-Book Value of Dow Industrials

CURRENT /	5 YR. HIGH /	LOW:	1 YR. HIGH /	LOW
2.43	4.37	1.13	3.00	1.88
	8/25/87	7/24/84	2/29/88	5/26/88

14. Price-to-Earnings Ratio of Dow Industrials

CURRENT /	5 YR. HIGH /	LOW:	1 YR. HIGH /	LOW
10.3	21.0	9.79	13.3	9.79
	10/6/87	11/16/88	4/12/88	11/16/88

15. Current Dividend Yield of Dow Industrials

CURRENT /	5 YR. HIGH /	LOW:	1 YR. HIGH /	LOW
3.53	5.05	2.58	3.80	3.33
	7/24/84	8/25/87	11/16/88	1/30/89

(Source: *Investor's Daily*, 2/13/89, p. 8)

By comparison, the above figures suggest that the current market does have some strength, even though other indicators are broadcasting signals of weakness. For example, notice the relatively low P/E ratio of 10.3 (# 14) reflecting the strong earnings which have existed for the past several months. The five-year statistics are brought up to date by comparison to the one-year statistics. The "psychological indicators" can provide a balanced view of the market move. This is a somewhat contrarian approach to a market move which has been sudden and is difficult to read in the main indicators.

Whether it is based on imprecise measurements, such as a gut feeling, or more definitive psychological measurements, the contrarian approach can be a reliable counterbalance to the market indicators. It must be remembered that the indicators and their signals are based on what has happened. They cannot determine what will happen, but rather will produce some signals as to what is likely to happen.

ENDNOTES

[1] Psychological Market Indicators, listed in the *Investor's Daily* newspaper.

Chapter Thirteen

Individual Stocks

In his writings, Charles Dow was reticent to recommend any particular strategy for choosing stocks. He did, however, make a suggestion of choosing a solid railroad stock which paid a good dividend. Today, this would probably be comparable to choosing a stable utility stock with a "good" dividend.

The fact is, it is difficult to come up with a generic method to recommend stocks. There are so many different kinds of stocks and so many different kinds of investors. Some of the investors are looking for income, some are more growth-oriented and some want to speculate. All of these investors, if asked, are likely to state that their objective is to make a lot of money. Most individual traders of stock are looking to have annual gains on their investments which are higher than the current fixed-income rates after inflation.

If an investor is going to make use of the Dow Theory and the stock market indicators, it only makes sense to invest in those stocks which are reflected in the indicators. Stocks which have a tendency to follow the trends of the Dow Averages can come from different places.

Obviously, a person can choose to invest in stocks which are a part of the Dow Averages, although there are stocks appearing in the Dow Averages which do not always follow the rest of the pack. At times, the market can be making a major move and these Dow stocks are doing nothing. Another disadvantage to investing directly in the Dow stocks is one of cost. These companies are some of the major corporations in the country, and the prices of the individual stocks can be quite high. An investor may want to find stocks which simply follow the movement of the Dow Averages.

All stock selections can be divided into three basic styles:

- Technical
- Fundamental
- Good Ideas

Each style has certain advantages and disadvantages.

Technical Stock Selection

Selecting stock for trading on a technical basis can be a formal "system" process, such as using point and figure charts. Point and figure charting is actually a fairly simple system of price charting, which uses a condensing effect in price movement. That is, the stock must move a certain distance in price before the change is noted on the graph. Other theories, such as the "Professional Tape Reader," chart the price movement of a stock in a sine wave. Whether a stock is purchased or not depends where the price appears on the "s" shaped wave.

A simpler, more informal, system can also be used. Charting price fluctuations to look for repeating patterns has shown some success in finding buy signals and sell signals. This system can also be used in conjunction with the Dow Theory and other indicators.

Levels of *support*, and ceilings of *resistance*, play a part in buying and selling stock, using technical analysis. These are the same type of levels, showing support and resistance, which were discussed in the chapter on the technical movement of the Dow Averages. The ideal short-term trade is to buy at a level of main support and sell at a level of toughest resistance. This assumes a certain amount of fluctuation between the two levels as shown in Exhibit 1.

Technical analysis of stock price movements, in the purest form totally ignores "fundamental" information, the analysis of a company's economic situation, earnings in the company or changes in the company's market position. Rather, it looks only at the price movement to give trading signals. It is believed that fundamental economic information confuses the picture and can invalidate the trading signals.

In order to effectively use the Dow Theory and other market indicators, some technical analysis should be used in selecting stocks for investment. An investor should be investing in stocks which tend to be up when the Dow Averages are up. When this happens, he should be looking for selling signals, and when the Dow Averages are down, looking for buying signals. Intra-day figures are good for this kind of analysis, although closing figures can be used. One or two days' worth of figures are not as meaningful as a month or even six months of figures.

The analysis can go into some depth. Comparing the moves of the stocks proportionately to the moves of the Dow Averages may provide some interesting insight, but it is generally unnecessary. The most important information to be learned from the exercise of comparative tracking is the matching of direction, whether up or down.

Looking at the one-week comparative chart in Exhibit 2 shows the need for tracking a longer time period. Of the seven stocks selected, only Unocal matched the Dow movement direction every day. Others, which are fundamentally similar to Dow stocks (Honeywell and Squibb), only matched the Dow direction for two of the five days. Even Alza, which is fundamentally quite different from the Dow stocks, matched three out of five days and was unchanged the remaining two.

Tracking stocks will bring a few surprises, but it must be done on a regular schedule for a time period long enough to establish a reliable information base. Establishing this base can be accomplished easily with a computer or referring to commercially available chart information.

The fact is, technical traders do better in some types of market moves than in others. We saw earlier how the long-term moving average and the advance-decline line tended to miss the turn in the market. If the turn was dramatic and sudden, these two technical measurements would take a considerable time to adjust to the new situation. If a market move from support to resistance is strong enough, the technical signals may be false.

Exhibit 1 Stock Price Movement Showing Support and Resistance

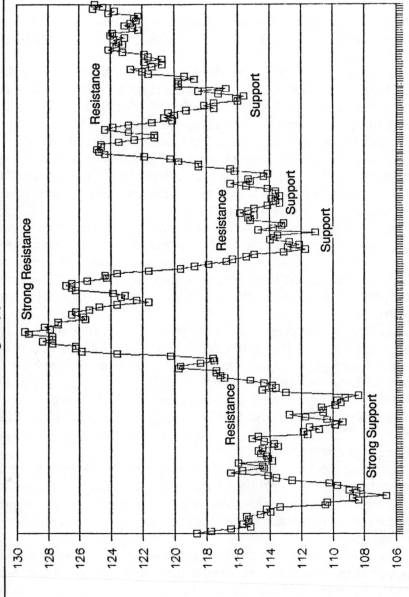

Exhibit 1 (Continued)

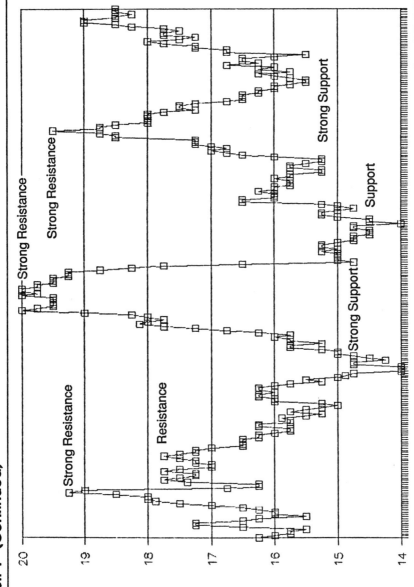

Exhibit 2 Technical Comparison; Stocks to Dow Industrials

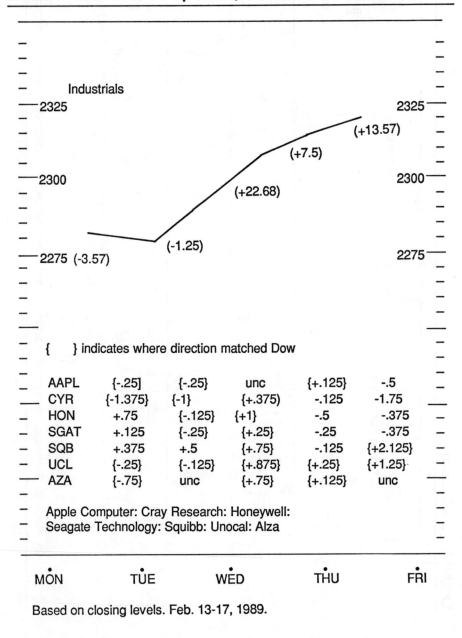

Industrials

2325 ··· 2325

(+13.57)

(+7.5)

2300 ··· 2300

(+22.68)

(-1.25)

2275 (-3.57)   2275

{   } indicates where direction matched Dow

AAPL	{-.25]	{-.25}	unc	{+.125}	-.5
CYR	{-1.375}	{-1}	{+.375)	-.125	-1.75
HON	+.75	{-.125}	{+1}	-.5	-.375
SGAT	+.125	{-.25}	{+.25}	-.25	-.375
SQB	+.375	+.5	{+.75}	-.125	{+2.125}
UCL	{-.25}	{-.125}	{+.875}	{+.25}	{+1.25}·
AZA	{-.75}	unc	{+.75}	{+.125}	unc

Apple Computer: Cray Research: Honeywell:
Seagate Technology: Squibb: Unocal: Alza

MON   TUE   WED   THU   FRI

Based on closing levels. Feb. 13-17, 1989.

The signals may all say buy, just as the market turns for a profit-taking correction. Conversely, the signals may be indicating sell, just as a new support level is established. This was the situation described in Chapter Twelve, where a contrarian approach was examined. In this particular situation, strength was found in the "psychological indicators" and to some extent in the "fundamental" analysis of the current economic situation. Fundamentally, corporate earnings were still quite strong, the current economic situation was essentially stable, and the psychological indicators tended to be neutral to bullish. The market stabilized and started a new rally.

The main weakness of technical analysis is a tendency for the signals to become more difficult to read as the market moves suddenly and with some distance. It may take some time for signals of strength or weakness to appear.

The main strength of technical analysis is the stock market's natural tendency to move in cyclical patterns. These patterns are often repeated and have indicators which give signals of strength or weakness. These signals are created by the actual buying and selling of stock. This is an active form of analysis which is looking at the immediate effect of all information regarding the stock market.

Fundamental Stock Selection

This form of analysis is based on the fundamentals of financial information relating to a particular stock. Fundamental analysis of a company takes into account the balance sheet, the profits or losses of a company, the amount of debt, tax considerations, market share, recent acquisitions, research and development of new products, recent happenings which affect future profitability, interest rates, strength of the dollar, and others.

The analysis can be extensive and time consuming. The difficulty lies in the fact that no matter how good the company may appear the movement of the stock is still dependent on how many want to buy the stock and how many are trying to sell the stock. This means that a certain amount of technical analysis is necessary to determine if the "fundamentally" selected stock has a tendency to move with the Dow Averages.

Fundamental information on companies can be obtained in several different ways. Many stockbrokerage firms have research departments which are staffed by analysis experts. They put out volumes of information on the fundamental analysis of individual companies. Some of this information is available at no charge, and some is available by subscription newsletter. The cost of maintaining these research departments is covered in the cost of the commissions charged on transactions.

The main advantage to this information is that it is usually well done and fairly easy to understand in its presentation. The main disadvantage can be one of the age of the data. If the information is a couple of weeks or a month old, the market situation may have changed. This disadvantage exists with any "research" information no matter where it is obtained. Age of the information can be a particularly troublesome concern where specific recommendations are being made on stocks.

If the stocks of individual companies are being recommended due to being undervalued, or are about to encounter an unusual event, such as their just having been awarded a big contract which will positively impact earnings, the information ages rapidly. The market will tend to react as the information becomes public. By the time the research report is available the news is too old to be of any value.

Information which retains its value for some time is the most basic fundamental data. Balance sheet information, sales growth, earnings, the amount of debt a company has, the dividend or growth in the dividend, the amount of institutional ownership are all types of information which can help the individual investor select a company which appears to be sound. Comparing this data to the Dow Average statistics can help the investor choose those companies which are likely to follow the Dow Averages and relate to other market indicators.

Take a look at Exhibit 3 containing a few "fundamental" statistics for the Dow Averages. Although there are many more statistics which can be examined, these will provide a basic example.

Exhibit 3 Fundamental Parameters of the Dow Industrials

Stock	12 Mo. HI/LO	Price	# Shares	Instiu.	P/E	EPS	Divi-dend	L.T. Debt.
Allied Sig.	36.875/28	32.5	148746	70277	11	2.94	Q 0.45	2002
Al. Co. Am.	56.0/51.25	56.0	88273	70660	6	8.77	Q 0.35	1809
Am. Expres	28.375/26.5	26.625	416460	249717	16	1.70	Q 0.21	12921
AT&T	30.375/28.625	28.75	1073750	243252	14	2.02	Q 0.30	7284
Beth Steel	24.125/19.25	23.25	74541	51410	5	4.23	Q 0.10	789
Boeing	64.375/58.25	60.625	153190	91461	13	3.80	Q 0.40	253
Chevron	47.375/44.25	45.75	342109	134855	9	5.34	Q 0.65	6244
Coca-Cola	45.25/42.375	44.625	357797	187201	16	2.72	Q 0.30	898
DuPont	89.625/80.75	88.25	239384	96119	10	8.85	Q 0.95	1106
East Kodak	47.75/44.375	45.125	324167	159663	11	4.10	Q 0.50	7956
Exxon	46.50/42.25	44.00	1307988	333276	11	4.01	Q 0.55	4908
Genl. Elec.	46.625/43.5	44.75	902953	427184	14	3.14	Q 0.41	3489
Gen. Motors	88.125/83.25	83.5	306025	126023	7	11.76	Q 1.25	15956
GoodYear	52.50/47.375	51.125	57246	37859	6	8.08	Q 0.45	3259
IBM	124.125/117.625	121.875	592127	288270	14	8.77	Q 1.10	5051
IntlPaper	46.875/43.625	46.375	111054	70361	8	5.90	Q 0.37	1775
McDonalds	48.375/46.00	48.125	188043	110711	15	3.31	Q 0.14	2763
Merck	58.75/55.75	57.75	393996	217994	20	2.86	Q 0.37	278
3–M	63.25/59.25	62.0	226180	145109	13	4.83	Q 0.53	408
Navistar	5.625/4.125	5.375	252090	114237	6	0.84	0.30	181
PhilMorris	102.0/95.75	101.875	230973	142944	11	9.58	Q1.125	5703
Primerica	22.50/21.125	21.50	96000	NA	8	NA	Q 0.07	3740
Proc&Gambl	87.00/81.50	87.00	169366	74881	14	6.23	Q 0.70	2486
Sears	41.875/39.00	40.875	378618	194914	11	3.84	Q 0.50	10059
Texaco	52.50/46.875	51.125	244312	103793	d	d15.47	Q 0.75	7695
USX	29.75/26.875	29.25	262098	139716	15	1.94	Q 0.35	6531
Union Carb	26.25/24.375	25.625	135837	80644	7	3.87	Q 0.20	2818
United Tch	41.625/39.125	41.125	130665	82473	8	5.21	Q 0.40	1643
Westinghse	53.75/50.5	52.625	143547	64383	9	5.56	Q 0.50	867
Woolworth	52.75/49.25	51.75	63886	36317	12	4.24	Q 0.41	328
			(000)	(000)	(12-mo. base)			(mi.)
			313713	142955	11	4.24	Q 0.48	4040
				(Average Figures)				

P/E figures were adjusted to 12-month earnings figures.
Source: S&P Stock Guide; Year End 1988.

Before examination, one might think that the fundamental data of the Dow stocks would be similar. After all, these are the companies selected to "represent" the stock market; they should be similar.

Actually, in order to be representative of the stock market, there should be stocks of various sizes and types. Notice the variance in the parameters. The fundamental of price has a high of nearly 122 dollars a share and a low of just over five dollars a share. The price/earnings ratio (P/E) has a high 20 with Merck and a low five with Bethlehem Steel. The debt for General Motors is quite high when compared to Navistar or Merck, on the other hand the earnings of GM are the highest listed.

These and other figures can be used to create a profile which can be compared to other stocks, not on the list. This is accomplished by creating a simple average. This analysis gives a starting point for comparison. Non-Dow stocks which have fundamentals similar to the Dow Averages may be likely to move in a similar pattern. The data for fundamental comparison is easily obtained, which means this technique can save time in selecting stocks for comparison to the Dow. The average figures of the Dow stocks can be used as a standard to which the basic fundamentals of other stocks are compared.

A look at the table in Exhibit 4 compares the fundamentals of seven companies to the average fundamentals of the Dow stocks. The similarities and differences are easily seen. Note that companies like Honeywell or Squibb come fairly close to the Dow statistics, whereas a company like Alza is quite different. This does not mean that Alza is not a good stock, it just means that it has different fundamental parameters, and, perhaps, will not follow the Dow Averages as closely as will other stocks.

Conclusions about the tracking of any stock must be made by actual observation. Fundamental analysis can give an investor a fairly clear idea of the strengths and weaknesses of various stocks and how this information compares to the Dow Averages.

Fundamental analysis also has a relative quality which takes into account the particular sector or industry in which the stock is a member. Some industry sectors tend to have higher P/E ratios, others tend to carry large amounts of debt. It can be worthwhile for the investor to carry the analysis a step further and compare the

Exhibit 4 Fundamentals Comparison: Stocks to Dow Industrials

	APPLE COMP.	CRAY RESH.	HONEYWELL	SEAGT. TEC.	SQUIBB	UNOCAL	ALZA
12-MO H/L	42.0/37.5	61.5/53.5	60.875/57.25	8.75/7.0	69.375/64.75	38.875/36.5	24.0/11.25
CUR.PR.	40.25	60.75	59.75	8.625	66.25	37.875	22.375
# SHARES	123022	30952	43113	49322	97026	116705	31383
DOW AVG.	313713						
# INSTIU.	79967	23113	32545	18230	59833	76891	14527
DOW AVG.	142955						
P/E RATIO	13	19	6	39	16	13	45
DOW AVG.	11						
E.P.S.	3.08	3.27	E 9.50	.18	4.11	E 2.90	0.50
DOW AVG.	4.24						
DIVIDEND	Q 0.10	0	Q 0.525	0	Q 0.40	Q 0.25	0
DOW AVG.	0.48						
L.T. DEBT	NA	108	730	307	69.0	4406	75
DOW AVG.	4040						

fundamentals of a company to those of the rest of the industry sector. This can be done individually, or it can be done by research into publications which make the comparisons. Spending some time in the business reference section of the public library can give the individual vast amounts of information for comparison. This can also be helpful in deciding which publications or newsletters may be worthy of subscription.

"Good Ideas": Stock Selection

There seems to be no limit to "good ideas" for investing in stock. Ideas may come from newspapers or magazines. They may come from watching investing-related television programs. Stock ideas are continually being promoted by stockbrokers, who all have a "different approach" toward meeting the investment needs of their clients. There are numerous newsletters available touting one "good idea" or another. Friends may suggest stocks they have made money in, during the past week. There may be rumors of takeover attempts on a particular stock. Just a little checking around can bring many "good ideas" to the surface.

Many of the "good idea" stocks do well, others have made their move by the time the information is out and are about to sell off. It can be quite difficult to determine just where a "good idea" stock is in a particular movement cycle. These idea stocks do have some definitive characteristics.

- The speculative nature of the move tends to make for high risk.

- The "good idea" quality is generally based on new information or rumor, the information may or may not be correct.

- There is usually a top price limit to the move; a level at which sellers will begin to unload their positions. This level may be reached before the expected top price is reached.

These three characteristics make "good idea" stocks highly speculative. However, some investors make a great deal of money with idea stocks. They should not be a total investment strategy, unless the investor can afford the risk involved. They can be a limited part of an investment strategy.

The investor can allocate a certain portion of investment assets specifically for speculative opportunities. Depending on a number of factors; risk tolerance, assets available, and portfolio performance, an investor might decide to risk no more than 10 to 15 percent of a portfolio on the ideas. This must be strongly adhered to if one is to limit risk and maximize returns.

Risk can also be limited by not waiting too long a time period for the "idea" move to develop. Although patience can be important for mainstream investing, it can turn vicious in a speculative play.

The following are suggestions for selecting "good idea" stocks.

1. Be extra careful with the following categories of stock.

    Penny stocks; these often have the highest risk and seldom have substantial rewards. It can also be difficult to obtain reliable information on these companies.

    Reverse split stocks; the reverse is usually done to increase the price of the stock. Often the price will continue to drop after the reverse split.

    Foreign stocks; it can be difficult to obtain reliable and current information on these.

    Highly volatile stocks; if a stock shows a 12-month high of 63 and a low of 3, the reason does not generally relate to the fundamental worth of the company. These stocks are possibly being manipulated, legally or illegally. Even if the manipulation was illegal, the investor is not likely to regain losses in a court battle.

    Investment announcements; when a large investor announces the building of a position in a particular stock (such as a corporation stating that they are buying the stock of another company "as an investment" with no intention of a takeover) the large investor may actually be ready to sell out.

2. Decide and move quickly. This can truly be a case of missing the move by indecision. Also, decide ahead of time at which price to take a loss or a gain. If the stock drops too low due to profit taking, is it best to take the loss, hold the stock, or

double up and buy more? These are all individual decisions, depending primarily on an individual's risk tolerance.

3. Accept the responsibility for taking the risk; the person suggesting the "good idea" probably has limited information. If an investor cannot tolerate losing money, this area of speculation should be completely avoided. If an investor blames the source for a speculative idea going south, it only leads to frustration and missing out on opportunities which are successful. Some defense can be found also in a quick check of the fundamentals of an "idea" stock. This can give an estimate of the degree of risk involved if the idea fails to materialize.

The selection of stocks to trade can be technical, fundamental, or idea-related. Investors can favor one technique over the others, or use a combination approach. Whichever approach is used does not matter as much as keeping the focus on implementing a strategy which, over time, is successful in achieving an investor's goals or objectives.

The analysis of stock movement and of stock fundamentals can greatly assist the individual investor in choosing stocks for which there are indicators giving signals of strength or weakness. Learning to accurately read the signals can allow an investor to maximize profits in stock trading.

Chapter Fourteen

Using a Computer

Many retail brokerages still display the electronic stock ticker with all of its difficult-to-read symbols, characters, and messages which flash by in an instant. Occasionally, stock traders can still be seen, gathering around the long flickering sign, their gaze fixed on the letters and numbers flashing by. People are often surprised to hear that the information appearing on the electronic ticker is actually ten minutes old or more. The story goes that the delay is caused by slowing the figures down so they can be more easily read.

Even though it is seldom used anymore for placing trades, new stockbrokers still learn how to read the information contained on "the tape."

Brokers who have been in the business for 30 or more years can still remember a time when employees wearing telephone headsets wrote current stock prices on a large chalkboard which could be seen by everyone in "the pit." Obtaining current, accurate price information depended on good telephone lines and the speed of those holding the chalk.

The advent of the computer terminal changed those slower systems for the better. Computer terminals at every stockbroker's desk are now able to get real-time quotes and other data. This improved information is a big advantage to the frequent stock trader. The stock quotes are more accurate and most definitely current. The computer screen even indicates the actual time of the most recent transaction.

Other basic types of information contained on the broker's computer are such things as the current bid/ask, total volume, high and low for the day and the last 12 months, the opening price, the previous day's closing price, and on which exchange the most recent trade was executed. The screen also contains the movement of various stock averages and indexes, volume traded, the tick and trin, the advances and declines, the most heavily traded stocks, the stocks which are showing the largest moves and other information available for analysis.

This information has proven to be valuable for the broker as well as the stock trader. As computers have become more commonplace, the services of the brokerage industry have adjusted to be more accommodating to the customer.

The individual investor can now access the same information available to the stockbroker. In terms of research and analysis, there is actually more information currently available to the individual stock trader than to most stockbrokers. The individual stock trader now has newswire information, instant charting of stocks and market trends, fundamental statistics on various companies, stock selection guides and the supreme power of actually placing orders directly on the computer terminal. No more waiting on hold to place a market order or waiting for a broker to call when he or she returns from lunch. Now the orders can be placed at the customer's convenience.

All of these conveniences come at a price. They are not quite the same as self-serve gas stations where a customer saves money by doing most of the work. There are still commission charges and the computer time is charged usually by the actual minutes used. It could be rather expensive to leave the office with the newsline running, using all those minutes of computer time.

The decision to make use of computers when investing should be based primarily on what is truly needed by the investor. Trading only a few times during the year probably wouldn't create much use for all the information services a computer service could provide. On the other hand, some benefit may be found in a self-contained system programmed with financial planning and record keeping.

A person who is constantly on the go and seldom in the office, may not be able to make use of an on line computer system, but may benefit greatly from a hand held quote machine: A device providing real-time market quotes and statistics throughout the trading day.

The frequent trader of stocks, who wants to be informed of the events currently moving the markets, is the ideal candidate for an on line computer system. In a moment, this investor has access to stock analyses, both fundamental and technical. Newsline information is readily available, as well as special news items concerning favored stocks. Current market statistics, as well as long- and short-term market forecasting are available to assist the investor in planning strategies. This can all be accomplished at the desk of the investor. It all comes together in giving the individual the ultimate power of actually placing stock trades from the computer. This is about as close as an investor can get to being one's own stockbroker.

For some investors, the computer can be a great asset. It is unlikely that a computer trading system will be perfect, but carefully selected according to needs and usage, the computer can be a valuable tool. The following is a brief analysis of three levels of service with which an investor can make use of computers to enhance stock trading activities. It should be kept in mind that the cost increases as the level of services expands.

First Level of Computer Service

Although many investors are not aware of the situation, there are computer services which are available at no cost, or minimal cost. These services are worth investigating, before making a large capital outlay for a new computer.

Phone-in Quote Services

Many brokerage firms have a special phone number which can be called for current market statistics and price quotes. The service may be as simple as a tape recorded message, or may be a touch-tone phone-activated service. There is usually no charge for the service and, in many cases, it is not even necessary to be a customer.

The services are set up to handle several incoming calls simultaneously, so there is seldom any wait for the information. The service may have a short commercial message, but this is a small price to pay for valuable information.

The simplest method for locating such a system is to check the phone book for an advertisement, or place a few calls and ask some firms if they have or know of such a service.

Ask a Broker

Many stockbrokers have access to computer services which are as good or better than those being promoted to the public. This may be a computer service provided by their firm, or one which they personally subscribe to for the use of their customers. In this situation, the cost of the computer service is covered by the commissions charged for the transactions.

Newsletter Hotlines

Some newsletters have toll-free phone numbers which subscribers can call for current updates. This service can help reduce the information lag-time which occurs between the event, the analysis, and the delivery time of the newsletter. This is a rather indirect use of a computer, but it has the advantage of having the analyzed information interpreted by the publisher.

Cable Television

The television is a computer terminal. Vast amounts of financial information are available through this computer. The information can be accessible on regular network programming, or through cable programming. The cable program also offers market statistics throughout the trading day. Access to this information may be enough for many investors.

Portable Quote Machine

In the past couple of years, this service has been spreading across the country. This is a service which provides a quote machine the size of a pocket calculator. It is battery-operated and operates on a radio signal. A monthly subscription fee will give the investor "real time" market quotes (not a 15-minute delay) throughout the trading day. This is an obvious advantage to the person who does not spend a typical day in one location.

The quote machine can be carried in a pocket or purse and easily referenced in an instant. This machine can be useful in tracking the market, market indexes, or individual stocks at any time during the day. This feature allows the investor to plot trends and look for intra-day signs of strength and weakness, which could provide excellent benefits in planning and implementing a strategy.

Second Level of Computer Service

The second level of computer use is more elaborate in receiving and organizing information. This may be a setup which gathers financial data from cable television and organizes the data onto a controlled format.

Computer Information Gathering

The main strength of a computer is handling information. Vast amounts of data can be assembled and controlled in the format of a computer program. Formats can be programmed into the computer to organize a daily input of data. The input can be performed manually on a daily basis, or can be accomplished by the addition of a modem. The modem can directly input the data into the computer, thus saving time and increasing accuracy.

Some investors have the background knowledge to program their own system for analysis using the data they have assembled. These custom designed programs can provide buy and sell signals arrived at from the formula on which the system is based. The display can look back in time and show how accurate the formula would have been for the past 200 or 400 days. The formula can then be adjusted, or fine tuned, until the trading signals most accurately match what actually happened in the stock market.

Exhibit 1 shows the product of a custom designed program which uses a formula incorporating up volume versus down volume over a specific period of time. The formula created the buy and sell signals and the graph shows the actual trading pattern.

Exhibit 1 Special Dow Technical Chart—DJIA

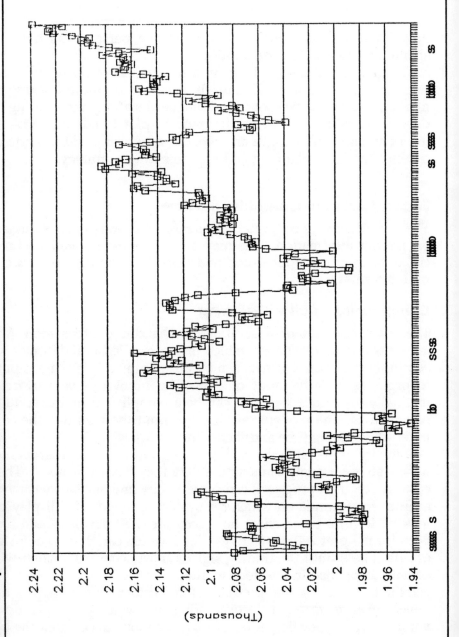

The graph of the Dow Jones Industrial Average in Exhibit 1 consistently shows the buy signals at the relative lows and the sell signals at the relative highs. The chart is a condensation of nearly 400 days.

The graph for IBM (Exhibit 2) shows a similar pattern, although a buy signal is missed rather early on the chart as well as the following sell. More toward the end of the time period, two sells appear, but the buy signal is missing. This graph seems to favor the larger price swings, and ignores the lesser movements.

The graph on Liz Claiborne in Exhibit 3 has a wider range of price movement. The formula appears to favor this factor. The first buy signal is a well-selected low, just before a magnificent rally. The following sell is well timed, just before the return to previous levels. The next buy is excellent, but the one after that appears to be premature. The next buy is missed totally, although the sell is on the peak. Then a premature buy, and another well-timed sell. Even though the signals are a bit inconsistent, trading to these signals could have been quite profitable for the 400-day time period.

This is an example of the kind of formula programming which can be done with computer knowledge, historic data, and a high-quality computer. The formula can be further adjusted and fine tuned to give buy and sell signals in a narrow trading range, as well as in the more major fluctuations. Like any system, it is not perfect, but it does have some consistency. One of the major weaknesses does not appear in these exhibits.

Like all forecasting, including the Dow Theory, accuracy becomes difficult at the extreme highs and lows. At the highs, this system will tend to give sell signals prematurely. At the bottom, it may give premature buy signals. The system tends to work best in a more steady market which has some fluctuation.

There are also commercially available analysis programs which collect and analyze market data. These programs receive data through a modem and can organize a complete trading strategy for the investor. Similar to a newsletter, this may be an information service which analyzes trends and produces buy and sell signals to the subscriber.

There are many computer program services available. There are services which will collect and analyze data, give buy and sell sig-

Exhibit 2 IBM Chart

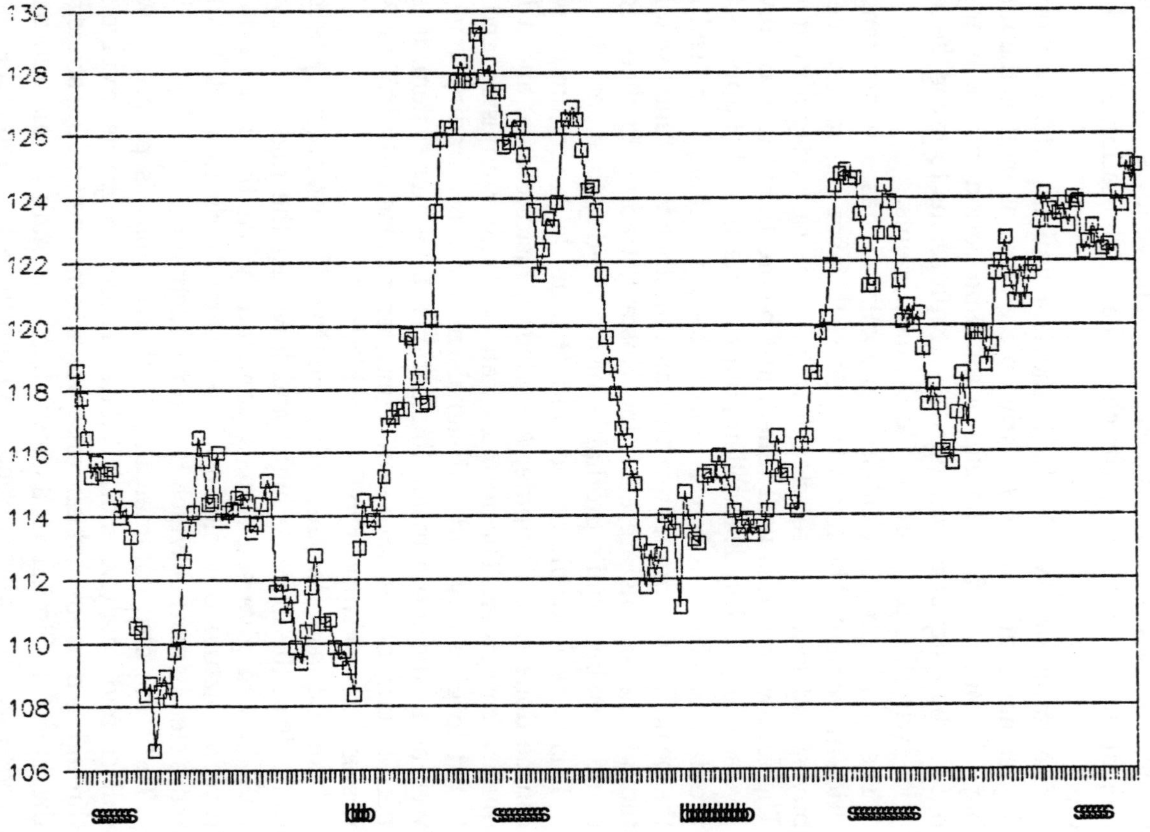

Exhibit 3 Liz Claiborne Chart

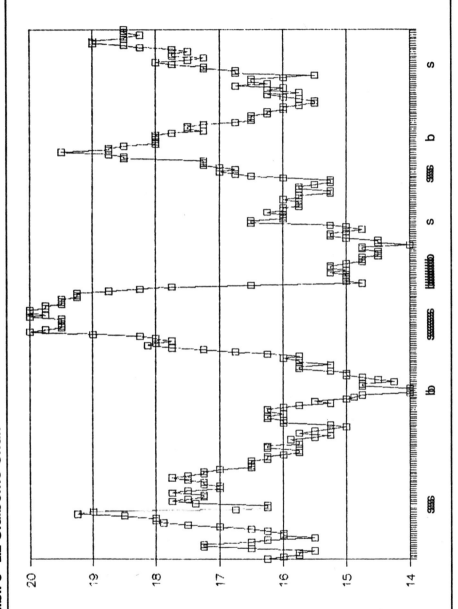

nals, produce charts and graphs; there are even services which will interpret the charts they produce.

The advertisements in the daily financial newspapers or magazines, will either have an 800 number to call for more information, or an address from which to obtain a brochure. Because the more elaborate programs are quite costly, it could be worthwhile to compare the features available to the cost of a particular system.

The consideration of three factors can lead the individual to the best system:

- *Need*: Which features are actually needed, and which features are just so many bells and whistles?

- *Quality Features*: Are the features available of such a quality that they will be useful, or is there something missing in a particular system?

- *Cost:* Is the cost of the system justified by what it actually provides? Will a less costly system work as well, or will it lack necessary features and information?

Many computer systems advertise a trial basis. It could be advantageous to try a few systems, in order to decide which one will provide the necessary service. Make certain, ahead of time, that the system can be returned. Also find out what charges will be incurred if the system is returned.

Third Level of Computer Service—The On-line Trading System

The ultimate trading system for some investors is a computer setup which provides current market information, current newsline information, stock analysis, market analysis, special situation analysis and the supreme feature: the ability to enter actual trades directly from the desktop computer. These features can bring professional resources and speed to the individual investor. If an individual is active in the stock market, an on-line financial system can bring these investment activities up to the level of the professional trader.

It should be noted that these services are in an early stage of development, and a certain amount of difficulty can be encountered. For example, it has been reported that systems can become overloaded during times of extra heavy usage. This was apparently true during the severe activity of October 1987. However, that time was unusual, as every trading system and communication line became overloaded. In most trading situations, the on-line systems work with efficiency and accuracy.

The following is an in-depth look at one particular on-line trading system. This particular system provides two levels of service (basic and supreme) to the user.

Basic Service

The basic account service is available at a running-time cost of 25 cents per minute and it includes the following features.

- *Account Information*: shows the current security positions, activity, and cash balances.

- *Credit Union Account Information*: shows the credit card, checking activities and balances in the credit union account which comes with the package.

- *Real-Time Quotes*: Market quotes, up to the minute. Extra real-time charge $15 per month. This is a proprietary service; without it, quotes have a 15-minute delay.

- *Evening Only Quotes:* This may be enough if the computer setup is at home and is not available at the office.

- *Special Research*: Special reports prepared by the firm's research department.

- *Special I.D. Number*: To control access to the system.

- *On-line Trading*: Orders are placed on the computer terminal. The telephone can also be used if the system is not functioning.

- *Newspaper Service*: Synopsis of a "popular" daily newspaper.

This basic level can work well for the frequent trader of securities. Just being able to access the account for an update of usable funds will save time and calculating. Placing the orders is probably the number one advantage to most investors, but access to quotes has a lot of advantages also. If the investor is near the computer during the day, the modest monthly fee for "real time" quotes could also be an important benefit.

Supreme Service

The full service on-line system has all of the basic level features and more.

- *Market Research:* An independent research program, providing stock selection and other helpful information.

- *Newsline Service:* Comparable to the newswire services used by professional traders. Up to the minute news on the market, stocks, and world events.

- *Analysis on Stocks:* Data analysis on more than 4000 stocks.

- *On-Line Special Information:* Reported insider trading and institutional moves.

The full package presents a fairly professional level of information and control to the individual investor. The cost has now risen to $1 per minute. To some, this would be quite expensive. It would probably not be worth the cost of entering three or four trades per year. But a person entering three or four trades per week or per day would find the cost reasonable.

The important factor is need. How much information is truly needed to conduct trading activities more effectively and efficiently? Is the computer the best source of this information, or can sufficient information be obtained elsewhere, at a more reasonable cost?

Research information at one's fingertips sounds great, but how much use will the information be a month from now or six months from now? The most usable features of nearly any "active" system are:

- The market quotes.
- The newsline service.

- The order entry capability.
- The account information: balance and holdings.

These features are the most useful because they are the information most immediately needed. They are the features needed as the investor is about to make a transaction.

Much of market and stock research can be done at other times. Times which cost considerably less than a dollar or more a minute. Notice, however, that the most usable features require the supreme package. The key to using the system efficiently could well involve a discipline of setting priorities as to the importance and timeliness of researching information.

Note: The American Association of Individual Investors, (AAII) has added an extra newsletter called "Computerized Investing." This could be a valuable resource in learning how to maximize the use of a computer for investment strategy.[1]

ENDNOTES

[1] The American Association of Individual Investors, 625 N. Michigan Avenue, Suite 1900, Chicago, IL 60611. (312)280-0170.

Chapter Fifteen

Putting It All Together

An investor can become familiar with the market in relation to the Dow Theory by working with the theory to chart hourly and daily movement. This can be done by using a computer or referring to a chart service, but the relationships between the different market moves appear with greater clarity and are more meaningful if the graphs are done by hand. When they are done manually, a person's attention and concentration are more intense than in reading a graph prepared by someone else.

When the graphs develop trends, noticing the confirmation and divergence of the averages becomes easy and interesting. Observing the areas of resistance and support, the investor can try some forecasting of the next day or the next week and compare these forecasts to what actually happens.

The investor will quickly learn and follow other indicators, looking for signals of weakness and strength. It is important to keep a record of the signals to see if they were accurate or false signals. The messages from the indicators can be compared to "gut feeling" in order to see which one is correct.

It is also important to remember that the Dow Theory, or any trading theory or system, can be incorrect at times.

Taking time to analyze stocks of interest to see if they move with the Dow Averages, and charting these stock price movements can also be a valuable learning experience in how the trend of an individual stock compares to the trend of Dow Averages. At the very least, the investor should analyze charts comparing stock price movements to the Dow.

Planned strategies should be fully implemented. A well-planned strategy will be the methods used to achieve the goals and objectives of a well-organized financial plan. The implementation of a particular strategy will take patience and time. If the strategy is not working, the investor should spend some time analyzing what the problems might be. The solution may be a minor adjustment to the strategy, or a new approach.

Ask for assistance. There are many brokers who are well-trained in areas of financial planning and setting strategies. Investors seldom ask for help, even though it is usually available.

One should take losses as necessary. This can be difficult at first. Taking a loss on an investment is not enjoyable for anyone. The question should be, can the assets be better allocated elsewhere? They may be put to better use in a different stock, a stock that will make up the loss and have more potential for gain.

Learning to take profits carefully can be difficult. There is a saying as old as Wall Street, "Cut your losses and let your profits run." Charles Dow referred to the saying in his writing, although it originated long before Charles Dow.

The question becomes, when should an investor take profits? This can be answered a hundred different ways, depending on the goals or objectives of the individual. If an investor is planning on trading frequently, profits should probably be taken as quickly as losses.

A Dow Theory strategy might be to take profits as a strong bull move begins to weaken. This appears to be the action taken by institutional traders. They do not necessarily liquidate their entire portfolios, but rather unload a portion. This action makes assets available for new opportunities.

Does the action match the strategy? It is truly amazing how some investors spend a great deal of time planning a stock trading strategy and get caught up in the trading frenzy of an unexpected move in the market. Strategy is soon forgotten and disappointment is often the result. Once a viable strategy is arrived at, take actions which implement that strategy.

The Dow Theory and other market indicators can be used in conjunction with other trading systems.

It is important to protect investments. One should never leave on a month-long vacation with a portfolio of stocks that is heavily margined, unless some form of contact is possible with what is happening in the stock market.

The events of October 1987 ruined a lot of vacations for people who owned a significant portfolio of heavily margined stocks when they left and came back to no stocks and significant debt.

There are many protective measures which can be taken. Reducing or eliminating margin debits, placing stop-loss orders and using protective-option strategies are some of the methods used to protect a stock portfolio.

Protecting an investment portfolio when leaving on vacation can take less time than it takes to load the car or pack the suitcases. Taking the time will help keep the vacation happy and carefree.

In the late 1800s, Charles Dow compared the stock market to the tides, slowly moving in and receding. William Hamilton later called the Dow Averages a "barometer," indicating the future economic developments of the country.

In the 1990s, the stock market will be influenced by the economic developments of the world. This influence will continue to make the stock market an arena for investment. The change and growth of the stock market will increase the variable factors determining market direction. The increase of the variables will make market forecasting more and more difficult. However, the stock market indicators will continue to send signals of strength and weakness. The Dow Theory will continue to function as it is based on the foundations of economic growth and development.

Changes in how the economy grows and functions directly impact the stock market. If a person is to manage an investment portfolio it becomes imperative to make active use of available resources. This is the only way an investor can hope to better understand where the market is and where it is going next.

GLOSSARY

The following are terms or phrases used by investors:

ARBITRAGE—When any market condition creates an inequality in values, whether real or merely perceived to be real (such as a rally in the Dow Transportation Average which occurs prior to a rally in the Industrial Average stocks), an arbitrage play would be to sell the perceived overvalued security (the Transport) and purchase the undervalued security (the Industrial).

ADVANCE/DECLINE LINE—An index of the number of stock issues advancing compared to the number of stock issues declining on the New York Stock Exchange. To calculate, an arbitrary base number is selected, then the total number of advances minus declines is added to the base if advances dominant, or subtracted from the base if declines dominant. Hence, the "line" moves upward if there are more advancing stocks and downward in the presence of a greater number of declining stocks.

ALL OR NONE—A qualifier on an order to buy or sell stocks (usually multiple round lots: 100, 200, 300, 1000, etc.) which states the order must be filled in its entirety, not partially. Although this qualifier prevents split fills, it can make it more difficult and time-consuming to fill the order.

AMERICAN STOCK EXCHANGE—A major stock exchange located in New York City. It was once known as the "Outdoor Market," or the "New York Curb Exchange," because trading operations were literally done outside on Wall Street and Hanover Street. Action on the American Stock Exchange can be an indicator of the interest of more "speculative" traders.

AUCTION MARKET—A market where goods or securities are sold to the highest bidder. Many investors forget that the stock market is, in fact, an auction market, where someone else must be willing to buy or sell the security at the customer's desired price and quantity. This is more the case in the buying and selling of options than stocks, which a specialist will buy and sell to keep the market "fair and orderly."

AVERAGING UP OR DOWN—A strategy where an investor makes additional purchases of a stock currently owned, thereby averaging the total cost. Many experts claim that it is less risky to average up than down, but both strategies can be effective.

BEAR—An investor or other person who believes that a stock or the stock market will fall in value. Sellers of securities, such as stocks or bonds are bears. A bear market is a declining market, where the primary trend is down.

BOOK VALUE—The computed value of a company if it were totally liquidated. Accuracy is often questionable due to assets which may be difficult to appraise at current value. Book value often has little or no relationship to the current market value of a particular stock. In some situations, the relationship between the book value and the current market value can be helpful in finding "undervalued" stocks.

BULL—An investor or other person who believes that the price of a security, or the market, will rise. A buyer of stock or other securities, or a description of a rising primary trend in the stock market.

CONSOLIDATION—A term generally used to describe a slowing of an advance or a minor market decline in an upward trend.

CORRECTION—A market decline which occurs during a bull primary trend.

CYCLICAL STOCKS—Stocks which tend to move with business cycles, whether lagging, leading, or concurrent.

DAY ORDER—An order to buy or sell a stock, with certain qualifications, which is good for that day only. If the order cannot be filled during the day in which it is placed, it is canceled and a "nothing done" is reported.

DEFLATION—An economic condition characterized by a decline of prices and a decline of business.

DISCOUNTING—A term used to describe a lack of activity in the market when activity was expected due to important news. The market is then described as "discounting the news." The market may have previously reacted in anticipation of the news, or there may be other news of equal or greater importance which causes a balanced market reaction.

DISCOUNT RATE—The interest rate charged by the Federal Reserve Bank on loans to member banks. The rate is a signal of a tightening or loosening of the money supply; therefore, it is an indicator of higher or lower interest rates.

DIVERGENCE—A term used to describe the market indicators which are giving opposing signals. For example, a divergence occurs when the Transportation Average is up for the day and the Industrial Average is down. Divergence can signal an approaching change in the strength of the current market trend.

DIVIDEND—Usually cash, although there are also stock dividends, paid by a corporation. Cash dividends are generally paid on a quarterly basis, although special dividends may be declared at times. Dividends are paid to shareholders who own the stock as determined by the "ex" date.

DIVIDEND CAPTURE—A strategy often seen in a slow, lethargic market which has investors (most often institutional traders) buying up large quantities of a stock just before the dividend ex-date.

EX-DIVIDEND DATE—The date which determines the recipient of a dividend. If a stock is purchased on or after the dividend ex-date, the purchaser buys the stock without buying the dividend. If a stockholder sells the stock on or after the ex-date, the stock is sold without selling the dividend. There are ex-dates for cash dividends, special dividends, stock dividends, and stock splits, as well as for distributions from mutual funds.

EARNINGS—The after-tax profits of a corporation. Often stated in terms relating to one share of stock, as "earnings per share."

EARNINGS PER SHARE (EPS)—The earnings of a corporation stated in terms of one share. EPS = total earnings / total number of shares outstanding. One of the factors used in "fundamental analysis."

EQUITIES—A term used synonymously with common stock. A reference to direct part ownership of a public corporation through owning shares of its stock.

EXCHANGE—A stock market, (such as the New York Stock Exchange, American Stock Exchange, or Pacific Stock Exchange) where "listed" stocks are purchased and sold for investors.

INFLATION—A rise in wages and prices of goods, and a corresponding decline in the value of money.

LATE TAPE—A delay at the stock exchange in reporting the results of transactions. A late tape is usually caused by abnormally high volume.

LIMIT ORDER—An order to buy or sell a security at a specified price.

LIQUIDITY—In a stock, liquidity refers to the ability to buy or sell the stock at will. There are low liquidity stocks which may only trade a few hundred shares per week. This can provide difficulties to the investor when buying or selling.

LISTED STOCK—Stocks which trade on the U.S. stock exchanges, as opposed to stocks which trade in the "over the counter" markets.

LOMBARD STREET—A financial district in London, similar to Wall Street in New York City.

MARGIN—Money borrowed from the brokerage firm, usually to purchase other securities. Interest is paid on the funds borrowed for each day the debt is outstanding. A level of ownership (equity) must be maintained and can result in a maintenance call (additional funds required) if the price of the security drops low enough. Required maintenance levels may be as low as 25 percent or as high as 50 percent in some situations. There are securities which are not "marginable." There are also safety restrictions which the individual brokerage firm can enforce for the protection of its customers or itself.

MARGIN ACCOUNT—An account with a securities firm, which a customer uses to purchase securities with margin (borrowed money).

MARKET ORDER—An order to buy or sell securities at the best available price.

OPTION—The right to buy or sell a specific quantity of securities at a predetermined price (known as strike price) in a defined period of time. Options are bought and sold by investors. For every buyer there must be a seller and vice versa. A call gives the owner the right to buy and a put gives the owner the right to sell.

OVER THE COUNTER (OTC) MARKET—Market in which securities not listed with any of the stock exchanges are sold. These sales take place between trading desks of various broker-dealers who act as agent or market maker for the transaction. Market makers buy and sell specified securities as principal and act as agent for those other securities in which they do not make a market.

PENNY STOCKS—Highly speculative, low-priced issues of common stock. Brokerage firms have differing restrictions on the trading of penny stocks.

PRIME RATE—The minimum interest rate charged by commercial banks to their best business borrowers.

RECOVERY—An advance in the stock market after a correction or down trend.

RESISTANCE—The point or level at which the price of a stock or a market index turns downward.

SPECULATION—The buying and selling of securities with the intention of making a profit. Speculation, like risk, is a matter of degree and is perceived differently by nearly everyone.

SUPPORT—A level at which the price of a stock or index stops falling; the level is then being "supported" by buyers.

SPLIT ORDER—An order which is filled in smaller blocks over a period of time. If the order is unable to be filled on one particular day and is carried over to the next day or beyond, additional commission charges may result.

STOCK AHEAD—A term which explains why an order has not been filled, even though the price may have reported on a particular order at the investor's limit. Other orders at the same limit were the "stock ahead."

STOP ORDER—An order to buy or sell a security once a trade has occurred at the stop price. The stop order then becomes a market order which is filled at the best available price. Buy stops are considered aggressive as they will only buy the stock as it begins to move. Sell stops are a defensive move used to protect against further losses. Stop orders should be placed far enough from the current price to avoid being filled on a minor price swing. The usual distance suggested is a minimum two points from the current price.

TRADER—One who buys and sells stocks or other securities on a regular basis.

TRADES—Orders to buy or sell stocks and other securities.

Suggested Readings

A Time to Be Rich, by Dr. Lacy H. Hunt. Published by Rawson Associates, 1987.

Dr. Hunt's book contains some excellent comparisons of economic cycles to investing cycles and even life cycles. In planning investments, the understanding of economic cycles can be as important as understanding stock market cycles. Likewise, just as there are times when an individual can afford to take risks and has the assets to invest, there are times in the life cycle when risk should be avoided. Acknowledging and understanding these cycles can help an individual plan the most effective investment strategy for any given time.

The ABC of Stock Speculation, by S. A. Nelson. Published by Fraser Publishing, 1964, first published in 1903.

This book, which contains the writings of Charles Dow, is uncanny in its relevance to the modern stock market. It explains the basis of the Dow Theory and gives the reader a sense of the logic behind the theory. This book can probably be found in the business section of any local library.

The Dow Theory: An Explanation of Its Development and an Attempt to Define Its Usefulness as an Aid in Speculation, by Robert Rhea. Published by Barron's, 1932.

Robert Rhea analyzed the writings and market wisdom of William Hamilton and published a book at a time when the stock market was heading for the bottom (1932). Rhea's analysis is substantial and objective as he points out the major error of 1926. The development of the Dow Theory, as quoted in articles written by William Hamilton, occupies half of the book and is truly interesting reading.

The Intelligent Investor's Guide to Profiting From Stock Market Inefficiences, by Dr. Robert Coulson. Published by Probus Publishing, 1987.

The stock market is efficient in a general sense, but often inefficient in more specific senses. Profits can be made in these "overlooked areas." The perfect example of inefficiency is the existence of the so-called "undervalued stock." In this book, Dr. Coulson does an excellent job of analyzing the market for special opportunities, classifying stock market behavior, setting models, explaining the "beta" factor and setting investment strategies.

How to Make Money in Wall Street, by Louis Rukeyser. Published by Doubleday Dolphin, 1976.

This book, which Rukeyser wrote more than a decade ago, is essentially as true today as it was then. Like his television program "Wall Street Week," the book is geared to the individual investor, addresses investments of any size, and comes across in easy, uncomplicated terms. Rukeyser is famous for providing information for the beginner, as well as for the experienced trader, and this book is no exception. It has something for everyone, including an analysis of the technical indicators or, as Rukeyser calls them, the "elves."

Finding the Next Super Stock, by Frank Cappiello. Published by Liberty, 1982.

Here, Frank Cappiello, a regular on "Wall Street Week," presents an excellent portrayal of "super stock" companies. He analyzes such "stars" as 3-M, Texas Instruments, Walt Disney Productions, and Tandy. The analysis is largely fundamental and provides an excellent, yet easily understood, analysis of potential "star-quality" companies.

Timing the Market, by Curtis M. Arnold and Dan Rahfeldt of Weiss Research Inc. Published by Probus Publishing, 1986.

This book provides a broad spectrum view of the use of technical analysis of the stock market. It delves into the basics, looking at such things as charting, trends and trendlines, reversal patterns, consolidation, gaps, retracement theories, support and resistance, momentum, moving averages, and on-balance volume. This is the ideal book for the investor who has learned just a little about technical analysis and would like to explore the area further.

Understanding Wall Street, by Jeffrey B. Little and Lucien Rhodes. Published by Liberty, 1987.

This is a good basic book for someone who wants a look at the history and development of investing and Wall Street. It is a combination of history, strategies, and definitions of trading in securities.

The Dow Jones-Irwin Guide to Using The Wall Street Journal, by Michael B. Lehmann. Published by Dow Jones-Irwin, 1984.

Michael Lehmann does an excellent job of relating the *Wall Street Journal* information to the ongoing study of economic trends. The book discusses business cycles, interest rates, and phases of business cycles, and relates profits to the stock market and leading economic indicators.

Panic on Wall Street, by Robert Sobel. Published by Truman Talley Books/ E. P. Dutton, 1988.

An historical look at Wall Street, with the focus on two vital areas: manipulation and panic. This book looks at the in-depth story behind various crashes, from the panic of 1792 to the major correction of 1987, and provides excellent examples of those who were able to manipulate and those who failed in them. The "myth" of the Great Depression is also explored, as well as the "power money" of Wall Street.

When to Sell, by Justin Mamis and Robert Mamis. Published by Simon and Schuster, Inc. (Fireside),1977.

This is an excellent book on technical analysis with consideration of other factors, such as fundamental and economic ones. It is a book based on experience rather than theory, exploring the Dow Theory and other indicators as if they are indeed signals. There is more depth to this book than the title implies and it is as valuable on the use of caution as it is on the use of action. Even if this book takes more than one reading, the effort is well rewarded.

One Up on Wall Street, by Peter Lynch with John Rothchild. Published 1989 by Simon and Schuster.

Mr. Lynch is the well-known portfolio manager of the mammoth Fidelity Magellan Fund. With a down-to-earth approach, this book looks at many aspects of investing in stock and is particularly good in the discussion of stock selection.

Investment Periodicals

AAII Journal, published by the American Association of Individual Investors, 625 N. Michigan Avenue, Suite 1900, Chicago, IL 60611. (312) 280-0170.

The Astute Investor, by Robert Nurock (technical analyst for the television show "Wall Street Week"). Paoli, Penn. (215) 296-2411.

Dow Theory Letters, by Richard Russell. Post Office Box 1759, La Jolla, CA 92038. (619) 454-0481.

Edison Gould's Findings & Forecasts, New York, NY.

Technical Analysis of Stocks & Commodities, Seattle, WA 98146-0518. (800)832-4642.

The publishers will send subscription information and sample publications on request.

Index